Law School

Without Fear

Strategies
for Success

Helene Shapo and Marshall Shapo

The Foundation Press
Westbury, New York

TEXT IS PRINTED ON 10% POST
CONSUMER RECYCLED PAPER

For Nat and Ben

*Our Children
and
Our Teachers*

Preface

This book began when one of our children decided to go to law school. It wasn't originally planned as a book. It just grew, out of conversations between us. The subject was what we ought to tell our son about ways to overcome the toughest hurdles that confront law students.

Year after year, with every new group of first year students, we see the same patterns of intellectual confusion and emotional tensions. As we talked about how to advise our own child about how to deal with both sets of problems, we began to put our thoughts into writing.

In introducing those thoughts, we want to tell you up front that at times you may feel that all you can do is to cope. You will think that the title of this book promises more than it can deliver. And in one sense you will be right. For many students, fear is part of the experience. When we were deciding on a title for this book, we asked several students for their reactions to the title we selected as well as several others. One mature and able student confessed that she was indeed fearful at the beginning and admitted, late in the spring semester, "I'm still scared."

Our message, however, is that you not only can cope with your fear and your stress, but you can overcome them. What we really try to tell you, beyond how to survive, is how to get the most out of your legal education. Besides being expensive, studying at an American law school is a privilege—and it is an opportunity.

Law professors ask a lot of questions, but they also at least suggest a lot of answers. As a famous professor once said, "Sometimes I asks 'em and sometimes I tells 'em." In this book, we mostly tell you.

How do you "tell" people how to capitalize this valuable opportunity? One of our fondest memories as parents comes from a long telephone discussion we had with one of our children in which we were making a forceful argument about how he should deal with a personal matter. He resisted everything we had to say. Finally, one of us said, wearily, "You're grown up now, a college graduate. All we can give you is our advice." Without hesitation, he responded, "Well, I value your advice."

We don't remember whether he took that piece of advice or not. We don't even remember what the specific issue was. That is not the point where this book is concerned. We hope only that after reading this book, you will value our advice.

Acknowledgments

This book has benefitted from the teaching of many people, but we must single out two. Those are our sons Nat, currently a law student, and Ben, a newly minted scientist. We learned from them even when they were children, we have learned more from them as adults, and they are a joy. During the final rewriting of this book, we were especially informed by Nat's experiences as a first year law student. Those experiences emphasized to us, even after all our years in teaching, just how much law school asks first year students to do.

The lessons of teachers since elementary school have enriched our understanding about how teachers impart knowledge and understanding. Our teachers when we were law students—at the University of Miami, at Texas and at Virginia—have focused that knowledge on the law. And our faculty colleagues—for both of us at Northwestern and for one of us at Texas and Virginia, have added immeasurably to our understanding of what makes a legal education. Our gratitude to them is itself immeasurable. We are grateful particularly to some sympathetic critics of parts of the manuscript: Larry Marshall, Linda Rubinowitz, Len Rubinowitz, and David Haddock.

We express our special thanks to Christy Bailey, our secretary, for seeing this manuscript through and for her cheerful and dedicated service over five years.

Contents

Introduction: How to Approach Law Study

The study of law is a fascinating pursuit. Along with your teachers, we welcome you to it. We are sensitive to the fact that many of our readers will be incurring substantial levels of debt to pursue a legal education. Knowing that, we want to emphasize our belief that you will find that your law school experience repays your personal effort as well as your financial expenditure. Besides being preparation for a variety of interesting careers, law study ought to be a stimulating experience. You will find downs as well as ups in the process. But we urge that when you get discouraged, you keep in mind the benefits you are seeking: not only professional preparation, but a considerable broadening of your general ability to analyze problems and a sharpening of your mind.

We have devoted almost a combined half century of our lives to the teaching of law, and in particular to the teaching of first-year law students. We have sought in writing this book to guide students as they begin the study of law. We aim to provide a framework for dealing with fundamental elements of law study that, on the basis of our experience, appear to be the ones that have proved most difficult for students to grasp. Many things we say in this book are, in one way or another, what your professors will say. In that sense, we are trying to reinforce their instruction.

Because law school involves learning both a new vocabulary and new forms of analysis, we provide what are sometimes simplified explanations of terminology, concepts, and analytical techniques. We hope these will help you to understand some foundational ideas and to go on to comprehend the more complex ideas that build upon them. We also seek, however, to help you make sense of an experience that at the beginning is frustrating for many, but should be fascinating if you approach it correctly. Thus, we set these ideas in the context of the psychological environment of law school—from which, you will see, it is difficult at times to separate the ideas and intellectual approaches of law itself. Besides focusing on the psychology of law study in an entire chapter—the last chapter of the book—we refer to it in several places throughout the book in ways that we hope will prove helpful.

Some of the ideas and techniques we identify can be learned only by constant exposure and repetition. Moreover, there is no substitute for mastering the details. We use many examples from courses found in most first-year curriculums—civil procedure, constitutional law, contracts, criminal law, property, legal writing, and torts. However, even as a reference, this book will not take the place of more detailed treatments of those subjects. We try here to do no more than give you a general framework that will aid your grasp of the law school curriculum.

We do believe that you will find it useful to consult this book for concise descriptions of ideas that recur throughout the first year of law school. Beyond that, we think that even in your exalted status as second and third year students, you occasionally will turn back to this little book as a refresher. As teachers and scholars, we hope that you will probe deeply into the concepts briefly presented here. Yet, we are mindful that sometimes students desire a highly directed catalog of the principles and ideas they are asked to learn. With that reality in mind, we have arranged the sub-headings in the book so that you may consult them quickly, perhaps sometimes even use them as checklists.

Our principal goals, however, go far beyond checklists. We are trying to present enough of an overview of law—at least the law that law schools present to their students—that when you get stuck in the trees of law school, re-reading this book may help you to see the forest. We also hope that on certain mornings during your first year of law study—mornings unpredictable in advance—you will wake up and suddenly understand what we meant when we explained something that you now have *learned*.

We want to emphasize here a point that appears in several ways later in the book. This is that studying law will teach you to ask questions and to analyze problems, but will not always provide clear answers. Many of your law school professors will not spend much time communicating clear legal rules, except to question them. The law student's lot is to live with uncertainty, and that can be unsettling. However, everyone goes through this experience. If you begin to feel troubled as you explore this new educational world, you are reacting normally.

A related observation is that there are a lot of lessons to be learned from law school that go far beyond book learning. The pressures of law school will reveal inner resources that you may not have known you had. Eventually, they will help you to put things in a more mature perspective. For many, law school will enhance a sense of community in a society where that sense is diminishing.

There are, moreover, some basic human truths that it is well to remember. Many students come to feel isolated in law school because of the pressures of time and the intellectual demands. Most first year students remark that their assignments—for classroom preparation and written work—usually take far longer than they would have imagined. If you understand that you are not alone in matters like these, it will bring at least two benefits. You will be able to reach out to others—for simple companionship as well as for academic help. But that understanding will also enable you to give help to others, which is a pretty good beginning for someone who is entering what is, after all, a helping profession.

Finally, you should not neglect your friends and your family. Try to explain to them the experience you are going through and the time pressures and emotional stresses it involves. Test out on them some of the problems that your professors put to you. Doing this even with those who are not lawyers—perhaps especially those who are not lawyers—will help them to understand your new environment. Their common sense often will help you to see approaches to legal questions you may have ignored. Moreover, you will maintain your connections to your life outside the law school environment, which will help maintain a balanced perspective about law school.

Aristotle told Alexander the Great that there is "no royal road to mathematics." There is no royal road to learning law, either. This book tries to help smooth some of the bumps.

1

Law: Constitutions, Legislation, and Courts

Overview

Legal philosophers spend a lot of their time trying to define "law," but most of the first year of law school consists of trying to understand some very basic practical aspects of the legal system. The principal elements of that study, which will occupy the bulk of your time, are the decisions of courts, which are an important part of our "law." But courts themselves operate in a broader framework of law, which includes constitutions and the laws enacted by legislatures—called statutes or legislation. This chapter briefly summarizes these three forms of law, as well as mentioning a fourth kind of lawmaking body, the administrative agency.

Constitutions

Constitutions represent the fundamental law of American jurisdictions. Where the United States Constitution applies, it outranks all other laws in the United States, including state constitutions, statutes passed by Congress and state legislatures, and court decisions. Within each state, the state constitution outranks laws passed by the state legislature and the decisions of the state courts.

An important practical consequence of the superiority of constitutions is that legislatures and judges must always try to insure that their statutes or decisions do not violate an applicable constitutional provision. An illustrative case concerning the constitutionality of legislation dealt with a federal statute that barred the shipment in interstate commerce of goods made by workers paid less than the minimum wage prescribed by the statute. The Supreme Court tested this law against the constitutional power of Congress to regulate interstate commerce and concluded that the law did not exceed that power.[1] If Congress had exceeded its constitutional power, the Court would have declared the statute unconstitutional and refused to enforce it.

The courts also test laws enacted by state and local governments for their constitutionality. A well-known example is *Brown v. Board of Education,*[2] a case consolidated from cases in four states in which the Supreme Court held unconstitutional provisions of state constitutions and statutes that required or permitted segregation of public schools. The Court concluded that these state laws denied African-American students the equal protection of the laws in violation of the Fourteenth Amendment to the United States Constitution.

The point of both these examples is that courts sometimes must consult the "law" of the United States Constitution, or of state constitutions, to determine whether a disputed action of state or federal officials—executives, legislators, or judges—is "lawful."

Legislatures

Legislatures—for our purposes, the Congress of the United States and the legislatures of the 50 states—enact law in the form of statutes. Other names for this kind of law are "legislation" or legislative "acts." Judicial decisions sometimes will refer to a single statute, for example, the Occupational Safety and Health Act, as "the Act." A comprehensive statute on a single broad subject may be called a "code." A familiar example, the Internal Revenue Code, is itself a substantial book.

---

[1] United States v. Darby, 312 U.S. 100 (1941).
[2] 347 U.S. 483 (1954).

Legislation, generally speaking, is superior to judicial decisions. This means that courts must enforce legislation even if they do not agree with its provisions, subject to their own judgment of whether it is constitutional. Legislatures may create rights that courts have not created, or expand on judicially created rights, or limit or abolish those rights.

A current example of legislative limitation of judicially created rights is the enactment of statutes that impose dollar maximums on the amount of damages that people suing for personal injury can recover for pain and suffering. Limitations of this sort are in turn subject to challenges as being unconstitutional. For example, injured patients who bring actions for medical malpractice might claim that a "cap," or limit, on pain and suffering damages in legislation that restricts remedies for malpractice is invalid. Contending that the legislation violates provisions of federal and state constitutions that forbid denial of equal protection of the laws, they would argue that the medical malpractice statute treats them differently from other personal injury claimants. A court faced with such a challenge would have to interpret the equal protection clause of the state or federal constitution and decide whether the legislative "cap" violates the right of medical malpractice plaintiffs to equal protection. If it finds the cap to be constitutional, it must enforce it, even if the judges on the court disagree with the statute as a matter of policy—even if they find it downright distasteful.

Administrative Agencies

Many statutes create specialized agencies to carry out particular tasks of regulation and other kinds of lawmaking. One function of these agencies is to enforce the provisions of statutes within their sphere of expertise. For example, the National Labor Relations Board's enforcement arm brings complaints against both unions and employers for "unfair labor practices," a phrase used in the National Labor Relations Act. Agencies also perform quasi-judicial functions. The judicial arm of the NLRB, for example, will initially determine whether an unfair labor practice has been committed. Courts will often review such agency decisions, interpreting the content of the applicable statute as it applies in a specific situation.

Administrative agencies also establish specific regulations, for example, safety regulations. In this way the agency enforces the statute by performing a rulemaking function, like a sub-legislature. Illustratively, the Occupational Safety and Health Administration creates rules about subjects as specific as how high guardrails must be. Again, courts will sometimes come on the scene. Frequently they must decide whether a regulation is an appropriate way to implement a statute. On occasion they must decide whether a regulation is constitutional.

The Court System and the Common Law

Trial and Appellate Courts

The United States has a well-developed, sometimes complicated, system of courts. This section provides an overview of the structure of that judicial system. We use the terms "case," "litigation," and "dispute" more or less interchangeably, just as courts and lawyers tend to use them. All these terms refer to a controversy between two or more parties that requires a court to make decisions on the facts and the law.

An important feature of judicial decisionmaking in this country is that it is part of a common law system. The common law is judge-made law: the body of law that emerges from the response of courts—principally appellate courts—to specific cases. The decision of a court on a specific controversy will exert a governing effect on other cases that present the same type of legal problem. That is, it becomes a legal precedent that courts in that system of courts must follow. Courts will then enforce this law that they have themselves made—known as the common law—just as they would enforce legislation. Americans may become so used to the concept of a common law system that we lose sight of the fact that in many countries only the legislature is the source of law. The courts in those countries enforce the rules of their legislative codes, but they do not create new rules. In the United States, the courts also enforce legislation, and their decisions in those cases constitute case law, but not common law.

Many times, appellate courts will develop a series of decisions on a particular set of legal problems. They will extend, modify and otherwise elaborate on the principle that they established in the earlier cases in the series. This method of step-by-step development—a favorite word of law teachers is "incremental"—is a principal feature of the common law.

The usual first stop for litigants—and for most litigants, the last stop—is the trial court.[3] This court performs a lot of sorting and screening tasks. It decides, as we shall explain, whether litigants are properly before it—whether it has jurisdiction.[4] If the court has jurisdiction in a case, then it must decide on both the law and the facts of that case.

Appellate courts exist principally to review the decisions of trial courts, when losing parties appeal those decisions. If an appellate court decides that a trial court made an error, it will reverse that decision, often sending the case back to the trial court for further proceedings. If, however, the appellate court finds that the trial court's decision was correct, it will affirm that decision.

In reviewing trial court decisions, appellate courts employ many tools. Their most characteristic function is to decide whether the trial court properly applied "the law." This law may include the common law—that is, the law developed through judicial decisions as we explained above. It may also include statutes and state or federal constitutional law, when the litigation involves those bodies of law.

Appellate courts also exercise some review over the judgments that trial courts make about "facts," that is, determinations about what "happened" or "occurred" that serve as the basis for the application of the legal rules we call the "law." Generally, however, appellate courts defer to the decisions of trial judges about the facts unless the trial court clearly erred. This is especially so concerning such matters as the credibility of witnesses. The theory is that the trial judge actually observed the witnesses' demeanor and can make better judgments about their truthfulness than can an appellate judge who is only reading a transcript.

---

[3] Some parties litigate in small claims courts, which we do not include in this discussion.

[4] See pages 7-9 below.

State and Federal Courts

Your course work will include a substantial dose of the work of both state and federal courts. Both systems have well-defined levels of courts.

State court systems feature at least one level of trial courts, most of which are courts of general jurisdiction—that is, they will hear all kinds of cases. Some state systems also include specialized trial courts for such classes of cases as criminal cases and family disputes.

Most states have intermediate appellate courts. These courts serve as the first place where litigants bring appeals. In states with intermediate appellate courts, litigants disappointed in those tribunals may be able to appeal further to the state's highest court. Each state has a "court of last resort," which is the highest court and which exercises supreme judicial power on matters of state law. Most states call that court their supreme court, although a few give it another designation. Notably, in New York, the highest court is the Court of Appeals, and the term "supreme court" refers to various lower courts. Frequently, the highest court in a state has substantial discretion about which cases to hear on appeal, unless a case is of a particular type that the court is required to consider, for example, a death penalty case. Often, a highest court makes a summary disposition of an appeal, with its judgment being reflected in a single word or phrase such as "appeal denied."

The courts of the *federal* judicial system hear cases that involve "federal questions," that is, issues involving federal statutes and the U.S. Constitution, and cases in which the United States is a party. Federal courts also hear cases between citizens of different states—called "diversity jurisdiction," explained at page 9 of this chapter.

Federal trial courts are called district courts. Appeals from their decisions go to twelve geographically defined federal courts of appeals, known as circuit courts. These courts have numbers from 1 to 11 (for example, the United States Court of Appeals for the First Circuit, usually simply called "the First Circuit") plus the United States Court of Appeals for the District of Columbia Circuit ("the D.C. Circuit"). The highest court, of course, is the Supreme Court of the United States, which exercises appellate review of decisions of federal courts of appeals as well as of state appellate courts on federal issues. Although there are a few types of cases that the Supreme Court must review, that court generally imposes a severe limit on its jurisdiction. It does that typically by its decision of whether to grant a petition for a writ of certiorari—a petition by which parties seek review—which it will do only a few dozen times a year.

The federal judicial system also includes some courts that specialize in particular subject matter, like the Tax Court and the Court of International Trade. You are likely to encounter decisions of these courts very seldom, at least during the first year of law school.

This is a simple chart, in words, of the court system. We want to emphasize that the jump from trial to appellate court on that chart is a big leap. Courts at all levels engage in sorting and screening functions. Among other tasks, judges are trying to do two things at once that often conflict—they are attempting to do justice to individual litigants, and they are trying to protect their courts' resources. Those resources become scarcer as one moves up the chain to appellate courts. For that reason, appellate courts tend to be rather guarded concerning the number of cases they accept for review, and the amount of review they will give the cases they do take. As much as they are able, they will try to interest themselves in questions of "law" rather than questions of "fact," and in the classification of emerging patterns of facts that allow them to state general "rules of law."

An important practical byproduct of the effort of courts to guard their resources—at all levels—is that most parties who bring cases to court will eventually settle them. They will work out compromises, frequently expressed in money, about their disputes. The alternative of settlement saves resources all around—not only the resources of the court, but also the time and money of the litigants.

Jurisdiction

Generally

The law of jurisdiction is extremely complicated. We simply wish to make a few basic points. The simplest observation is that one does not just come to court and get into court. One has to convince the court that there is a law—the law of jurisdiction—-that requires it to hear a case.

For our present purposes, jurisdiction refers to the power, that is, the authority, of a court to adjudicate a dispute. A court's jurisdiction first is limited geographically to the area in which it can enforce its decisions. A state supreme court, for example, can enforce its decisions only within that state.

Other fundamental forms of jurisdiction are jurisdiction over the "subject matter" and jurisdiction over a person or thing. To establish jurisdiction over subject matter in both state and federal courts, a party generally must show that the court has power to hear and decide a controversy under an applicable constitutional provision, or statute, or a judge-made (common law) rule. In many cases it may be relatively easy to establish this subject matter jurisdiction. For example, a few lines in a complaint that identify an alleged breach of contract, a subject covered by common law and statutory rules in each state, may serve to convince a court that it has jurisdiction to hear the case. Other cases may present knotty problems as to whether there is a basis in legal rules for the court to consider the case, for example, whether a state court has jurisdiction over a case involving certain federal statutes.

The books are full of complicated questions involving personal jurisdiction. These include, for example, issues concerning jurisdiction over out-of-state parties—including individuals and corporations—whose links with the court in which suit is brought are arguably tenuous. Illustratively, a court may have to decide whether it has jurisdiction over a company whose allegedly defective product caused injury in that state even though it had no office or factory there and did not actively market the product there.

It is also worth noting that sometimes courts exert jurisdiction over things rather than persons—called "in rem" jurisdiction. This often happens when a governmental agency seizes an object, or group of objects. One of our favorite examples is the case, *United States v. 1,500 Cases More or Less, Tomato Paste,*[5] in which the government alleged that the product was adulterated under the definitions in the

---

[5] 236 F.2d 208 (7th Cir. 1956).

Food, Drug and Cosmetic Act. Of course, the cases of tomato paste are not the operational defendant. They need a lawyer, and it will be their owner who provides one. Yet the owner is not the defendant in the eyes of the law. The outcome of the litigation will not be, for example, to send the owner of the tomato paste to jail, but it may well be to transfer title from the owner to the government, which will confiscate the adulterated products.

Our general point concerning jurisdiction is that one does not obtain a hearing from a court just by walking through the doors of a courtroom. A litigant must establish jurisdiction, and sometimes one of the litigated issues is whether the court has power to judge the dispute.

Federal Diversity Jurisdiction

An important jurisdictional power of federal courts embraces cases involving citizens of different states. This "diversity jurisdiction"—the "diversity" being the difference in the state citizenship of the litigants—involves a rather technical body of law that you will study in your civil procedure class. Diversity cases involve litigation over state law issues, yet the federal courts must hear these cases because Article III of the U.S. Constitution requires that they do. There are various limitations on this jurisdiction, including dollar minimums for the value of cases, and some rather subtle refinements to it; there are also frequent proposals to do away with it or to limit it severely. Our basic point is simply that when one sees that parties to a dispute come from different states, one naturally considers the "diversity" route into federal court. The existence of diverse citizenship does not mean that a controversy will automatically wind up in federal court—only that it may. Whether a dispute settles into federal or state court often depends on strategic choices made by lawyers.

A significant consequence of the diversity jurisdiction, which will be an assumed part of many cases you will read, is that in diversity suits between citizens of different states, the federal courts will apply certain state legal rules. Specifically, this is so with respect to rules of "substantive" law—for example, the rules of tort and contract—although not with respect to rules of procedure, which are provided in all federal cases by the Federal Rules of Civil Procedure.

Different Kinds of Law

Civil and Criminal Law

A fundamental distinction between types of cases is that between civil litigation and criminal prosecutions. The parties in civil cases most frequently will both be private parties, either individuals or corporations, alth ugh sometimes one party in a civil case will be the government. The plaintiff in a civil case initiates the action with a complaint. This legal document will explain the plaintiff's grievance and seek a remedy, asking the court to force the defendant to pay money to the plaintiff, or, in some cases, to do or stop doing something. Even if the government is a party to a civil case, it may be treated as if it were a private person. If, for example, a government driver has a traffic accident, the government as the driver's employer will be held vicariously to the same standard of conduct of any private employer.[6]

By contrast, in a criminal case, there is no plaintiff. The government always initiates the litigation; it is the prosecutor. It acts on behalf of the state or the commonwealth, or the United States. The victim of a crime obviously is a party to a criminal proceeding in a moral sense, and frequently will testify as a witness; yet the government does not sue on behalf of the victim, but rather on behalf of "the People." The victim is not a party to the prosecution.

Moreover, the government as criminal prosecutor acts with consequences that are often different in kind from normal civil litigation. The most striking potential difference is that many crimes involve the possibility of imprisonment. It is true that some successful criminal prosecutions will lead only to money payments made to the state, commonly called "fines," rather than to a jail sentence. It is also true that some regulatory actions involve civil fines, and thus the categories are not airtight in either direction. An important point, however, is that usually there is a stigma of guilt associated with a criminal conviction, whether it leads to imprisonment or only to a fine.

---

[6] We will not discuss here the complexities of an important exception that applies when the government acts in a "discretionary" way.

This distinction explains why the term guilt is not technically appropriate for civil litigation. Of course, in ordinary conversation, we may casually use that terminology in the context of civil cases. As a matter of careful usage, however, it is probably better to reserve the idea of guilt for crime rather than for the civil wrongs called torts or for breaches of contracts. In legal parlance, defendants in those cases will be "liable" if they lose the litigation, but not "guilty."

It is very possible for a particular kind of conduct to render an actor vulnerable to both criminal prosecution and civil litigation. Thus, someone who physically assaults another might be called before Judge X in a criminal prosecution on Monday for the crime of aggravated assault. And the same person might be a defendant before Judge Y in a civil suit for battery brought by his victim and tried in another courtroom in the same courthouse on Thursday. Accusations that O.J. Simpson killed his ex-wife and another man provide the most celebrated recent example. Simpson, acquitted of murder charges, later faced civil liability suits for "wrongful death," a tort action.

"Private Law" and "Public Law"

Your teachers sometimes will refer to "private law" and "public law" as relatively distinct categories. These classifications are not air-tight, but you should be sensitive to the fact that lawyers, especially academic lawyers, may perceive a distinction between them.

The classic "private law" subjects for first-year students are torts, contracts, and property. These subjects encompass law that principally emerges from disputes between private individuals. The focus, typically, is on resolving a particular controversy within a set of rules evolved for the purpose of dealing with private disputes. The basis for these rules often is the common law, although there are now many statutes that supply the governing law—for example the Uniform Commercial Code applies to many contract cases.

Some of the great "public law" areas, which invariably involve governmental bodies, are subjects like administrative law and other regulatory law. The public law subjects usually find their roots in legislation. In fact, their purview is as broad as the statute books.

Court decisions in the public law area represent judicial efforts to resolve disputes about such questions as the meaning of statutes, and whether regulations promulgated by administrative agencies fit within the purpose of the statutes under which they were issued.

Courts dealing with problems of this sort do not start with rules that they have developed themselves—that is, common law. They begin, instead, with political expressions of the will of the community—the enacted law called legislation and the even more supreme expressions called constitutions. When questions arise about the interpretation of legislation, the main issue usually is what the legislature, acting on behalf of the political community as a whole, should be taken to mean by a statute. In the public law arena, courts often resort to procedural devices and rules of statutory interpretation, discussed below,[7] which may tilt a hard-fought dispute one way or another. One must emphasize, however, that when fulfilling this role, courts generally are not supposed to act as the guardians of the community's political or moral views—only as interpreters.

When you study public law and statutes generally, you should keep in mind how powerfully some legislation manifests the deeply held views of the electorate. Consider legislation as technical as the Internal Revenue Code. The rates of taxation it sets, the exemptions it creates, the deductions it allows—all these represent highly political declarations of preference about such matters as the distribution of wealth in society and the desirability of particular activities. The tax rules of the Code affect individuals' incentives to create new businesses, to accumulate wealth, even to enter into marriage.

Other kinds of legislation do not even mask their social purposes: statutes prohibiting discrimination on the basis of race and gender, laws restricting the conduct of both employers and workers in labor disputes, legislation requiring notification of the parents of minors seeking abortions. When you deal with the rules embodied in statutes of this kind, you know you are dealing with "public law."

It has been observed that even "private law" has "public law" aspects.[8] Once courts employ notions of public policy in judging private disputes, explicitly taking into account the broader consequences of their decisions, they are importing "public" characteristics

---

[7] See pages 68-76.
[8] See, e.g., Leon Green, Tort Law Public Law in Disguise, 38 Tex. L. Rev. 1 (1959); 38 Tex. L. Rev. 257 (1960).

into private law. Nevertheless, most people would still maintain the broad distinction.

Private Institutions as Lawmakers and Uniform Laws

Generally

This chapter about "the law" has devoted itself principally to rules that come from constitutions, legislatures, courts, and agencies—rules that have some sort of binding effect on people who make decisions about how to conduct their activities or who bring disputes to court.

There are, however, various private organizations that contribute to the making of legal rules—sometimes with great influence. For example, industry trade associations and other institutions publish standards to guide, or even dictate, the conduct of their members. Such organizations may articulate requirements that apply to various kinds of activities, ranging from professional behavior to standards for the design of buildings or products. Thus, a private medical or hospital organization may set standards for the behavior of medical personnel in particular situations involving hospital patients. Or an association of swimming pool manufacturers may declare that all swimming pools must display pictographs that warn of various hazards that swimmers face.

Law students will become familiar with at least two collections of rules that have exerted particular influence on judicial and legislative lawmaking. These are the Restatements of the Law and the legislative proposals of the National Commissioners on Uniform State Laws.

The Restatements

The organization that publishes the Restatements of the Law is the American Law Institute (ALI), a private organization made up of approximately 3,000 lawyers, including judges, practicing lawyers, and law professors. Restatements seek to present comprehensive sets of rules that cover important areas of the law. The goal is to provide guides for judges when they deal with questions on which their jurisdiction has not yet ruled, or concerning which they are in doubt.

The Restatements you are most likely to meet in the first year of law school are the Restatements of Torts, Contracts, and Property. All of these are multi-volume works. It would be useful to pick up one of them in the reference section of the library and skim through it.

The usual style of Restatements is to present a bold-faced rule—called the "blackletter"—that covers a recurrent pattern of situations, followed by comments and illustrations that justify and explain the rule. For example, the sections of the Restatement of Torts that deal with the law of false imprisonment define this tort by setting out its basic elements—for example, the requirement that a plaintiff claiming false imprisonment must show that she was completely confined and that the defendant acted intentionally to confine her. The blackletter sections also spell out various ways in which a defendant may effect a confinement, including physical barriers, threats, and other forms of duress. The illustrations provide fact-based examples that spell out the meaning of the blackletter—for example, explaining that a threat to shoot a person's child if she leaves the room is a form of duress that effectively achieves an imprisonment.

Although most Restatement rules represent consensus views about the law, some may represent choices made by members of the ALI on rather controversial matters. In this regard, it is important to remember that the force of the Restatements principally comes from their power to persuade. Since the ALI is a private organization, it has no lawmaking power. A Restatement section becomes binding law in a jurisdiction only if its courts adopt it. Thus, a court's acceptance of a Restatement rule on a novel question represents, at least in theory, its acceptance of a reasoning process. That is why the comments and the illustrations to Restatements are important; they help to give flesh to the bare rule of the blackletter.

Uniform Laws, Including the Uniform Commercial Code

The codes and rules published by the National Commissioners on Uniform State Laws have a different goal than the Restatements. Rather than providing a statement of principles to guide judges, uniform codes and acts seek to present comprehensive legislation for adoption by state legislatures.

The uniform law that you will encounter most regularly in your first year will probably be the Uniform Commercial Code (UCC). The UCC deals with a wide range of commercial transactions, from lending transactions involving the use of chattels for security to everyday banking business. The sections you will most likely confront in the first-year Contracts course are those dealing with sales—Article 2 of the UCC. The many sections of that article provide rules on such subjects as when an offer may be considered to have lapsed, when oral agreements become contracts, and what rules should be applied when a contractual term is left open.

The hope of the drafters of uniform laws is that they shall in fact be uniform: that all states will adopt them. Indeed, this is what has happened with the UCC, although some states have created exceptions to certain provisions and, with respect to a few particularly controversial subjects, the commissioners have provided state legislators a set of alternative provisions.

It bears emphasis that a uniform law or code is not a law until a legislature enacts it. Despite its name, it represents a draft offer of a statute, made to legislatures by the Commissioners. Like the Restatements, it depends on its power to persuade. That persuasive force comes from the reasoning that supports the many provisions in the uniform law as well as from the idea of its comprehensiveness, and the hope that it will be truly uniform across the country. Thus, uniform laws depend in part on a political argument—that legislators who may be opposed to specific provisions in a uniform law should swallow their opposition in order to serve the greater goal of uniformity.

2

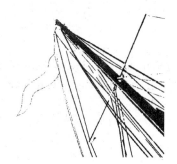

Briefing a Case

Most teachers of first-year courses will ask you to "brief" cases, that is, to write a summary and evaluation of the judicial decisions you read for class. There is nothing mysterious about this process. It breaks down into a few categories that, with practice, will become understandable. Various instructors will use slightly different terms to label these categories. Your first rule in that regard is, humor the particular instructor's preferences. The categories we employ, however, are in fairly widespread use and should give you a starting point for briefing cases.

The process is one that is basic to lawyers' work. It requires the person doing the brief to take apart a case—to analyze its facts and the law that the court applied in a procedural context, and to explain the reasons for the decision. At a minimum, case briefs will help you prepare for class, and many first-year students use them for that purpose. Beyond that, the repeated practice of briefing will give you a feel for the legal profile of cases.

The Facts

The first element of a brief usually is the facts. The appellate cases that form the basis of many first-year coursebooks usually squeeze into a few paragraphs what the appellate court thinks are the relevant facts. Students who have worked in law offices know that these capsules of the "facts" sit atop what may be roomsful of documents and stacks of testimony. But for the purposes of assignments based on appellate decisions, the student must concentrate on the facts as the appellate court sets them out.

The best way to learn how to summarize the facts of a case is to do it several dozen times, if not several hundred times. We will provide a few examples and hints, but perhaps the most important part of stating the facts—as it is an important requirement in the law generally—is to be relevant. The quest for relevance, as it applies here, means that after reading and re-reading a case, you must identify the facts the court found important for the ruling it made about the law.

An example of facts that may differ in their relevance in particular cases concerns matters related to the personal characteristics of the parties. Thus, for example, the age of a plaintiff suing for personal injury—even if the court mentions it—may not be at all important to the applicable law. The crucial legal questions on appeals of personal injury cases typically would involve how the defendant behaved and the manner in which the plaintiff suffered injury. However, in some cases, the age of the plaintiff may be crucial. For example, some states have a doctrine (sometimes called the "child trespasser" doctrine and sometimes labeled with the term "attractive nuisance") that effectively raises the standard of care that landowners owe to young visitors to the land. In a case of that sort, obviously the plaintiff's age would be relevant. The age of a plaintiff would also be relevant to a court's determination of the amount of damages; a disabled plaintiff's life expectancy is a key factor in the question of how much earnings he has lost because of an injury.

Another example of a fact with differing properties of relevance would be the race of a party. To identify a party by race in an ordinary contract action, for example, would be to waste words. But in a civil rights case that turned on a business establishment's refusal to serve a potential customer, the fact of race is crucial.

One practical hint for both your routine preparation and any recitation you may give in class is, don't be wooden. That is, do not just write out the "facts" by using the exact words the court used (unless there appears to be a particular reason to do that). Do the brief in your own words. This will force you to understand what the case is about. It may even impress your teacher.

The Procedural Context

It is important that you understand the procedural framework of the case, because the procedural context in which the court decides the case is often critical to your analysis of the court's decision. Different instructors may ask for the procedural context in different ways. We give some brief explanations of main procedural checkpoints in Chapter 4.

At this point, we simply note that there are a few terms that usually will signal the trial court context from which a case came to the appellate court. This list is not exhaustive, but appeals from decisions on these motions probably cover nine cases out of ten that you will read:

- The motion to dismiss (or §12(b)(6) motion in federal cases) (or demurrer) (or nonsuit)
- The motion for summary judgment (or Rule 56 motion in federal cases)
- The motion for directed verdict (or motion for judgment as a matter of law) (or instructed verdict)
- The motion for judgment notwithstanding the verdict (judgment n.o.v.) (or motion for judgment as a matter of law after trial)
- The motion for a new trial

You also will encounter the concept of appeal itself, and mechanisms such as the petition for a writ of certiorari and "certified questions," which, besides direct appeal, are other principal ways to get into appellate courts.

Our main point here is that you must be sensitive to the fact that cases have histories when they arrive at appellate courts. Those histories are not just the human stories of the case, although that may be very important. They include the legal packaging in which the case came to the court. One must read appellate decisions in the context of the trial court's decision, including its procedural frame-work. Did the case get to a jury? If it did, then the plaintiff overcame the defendant's motion to dismiss and/or motion for summary judgment, and also probably survived a motion for directed verdict. Even if you do not understand the procedural terminology at first, seize on it and try to relate it to the eventual disposition of the case.

The Issue

The issue is the point that the litigants are disputing. Different people will suggest varied ways to state an issue. We suggest that you think of an issue as a question, a *legal* question that relates to the facts of the case in a somewhat abstract way, and which the court must answer. Your statement of the issue should explain the question in one sentence understandable to someone who has not read the case.

Here is an example of an issue. Assume that the law attaches certain consequences to calling an act a battery. Assume that within a particular jurisdiction (a state court) the courts define battery as an unconsented act, done with the intent of bringing about a harmful or offensive contact with the person of another, which causes such a contact. Assume that Jones walks up to Smith as Smith is waiting in line, holding a tray, at a buffet at a business meeting lunch. Jones snatches the tray from Smith's hands and yells at him that he wasn't invited to the meeting or the lunch. Smith is humiliated. He sues Jones for a battery. After the evidence is heard, the trial judge grants a directed verdict against Smith, reasoning that since Jones did not touch Smith's person, no reasonable person could find that Jones committed a battery. Smith appeals.

Here is one way to state the issue: "Does a person commit a battery when he pulls an object from another person's hands in an insulting way, but does not touch the body of the other person?" Here are some reasons that this sentence is a good issue: It is in one sentence. It is an interrogative sentence—it actually asks a question. It can be understood by someone who has not read the case. It relates to selected facts that are stated somewhat more broadly than the particular facts of the case at issue. It begins by identifying the legal claim involved and then moves to the facts. It lays bare a legal problem (whether the defendant must have directly contacted the plaintiff's body) that requires the court to make a statement of law that resolves the problem (that a person can commit a battery by indirect contact, that is, by touching an object connected to the plaintiff's body). You could also present the facts in this statement of the issue as "when he pulls a tray from another person's hands and rudely yells at him." This sentence states the facts narrowly, using the exact facts of the case.

Whichever one of these formulations you prefer, you should consider, by contrast, this example of how not to write an issue: "was the defendant's action a battery?" This question does not include any facts of the case. Saying "the defendant's action" (or, "Mr. Jones's action") does not help the reader to understand the issue. The specific legal problem is whether a contact with an object that the plaintiff was holding is a battery. Moreover, identifying a party as the defendant does not help either. There is always a "the defendant," and that designation does not help solve the legal issue. Moreover, the actual names of parties are almost invariably irrelevant, and too specific. Although there are often times when you may identify parties by names (when you write memos for law firms, for example), in case briefs and in your legal writing assignments it is better to identify parties more generally.

You can now see that it becomes important to decide how to identify facts, especially how broadly or narrowly to identify them. You state facts broadly by using abstract or general terms rather than concrete or specific ones. Abstract words are those that express qualities and ideas; concrete words refer to actual things, that is, specific objects. Much written and oral communication in law school will require you to go from the abstract to the concrete and vice versa. Frequently, you will be both expressing abstract ideas and explaining them through concrete examples.

A related distinction is that between the general and the specific. A general term refers to a group or a class of people or objects. A specific term refers to a particular member of the group. Usually, an issue should tend towards general terms. In the battery example "a tray" is specific; "an object from another person's hands" is more general, and is a broader description of the facts because it encompasses more items than does the specific noun "tray." To take another example, assume that a case involves a store alleged to have advertised products at a very low price when it did not have any in stock, simply to lure customers. You might specifically cast the issue by using the name of the defendant: "Must Payless Stores provide the product at its advertised price to a customer who did not find it in stock?" The defect of this issue is that the reader has insufficient information about its factual background. It might be legally more helpful to identify that defendant more generally by its relationship to the claim, for example, as a store that advertises. Note how this statement of the issue defines it better: "Has a store that advertises a product at a particular price made an enforceable offer if the product is not in stock?"

It is often difficult to decide just how broad or narrow to be. That decision often depends on the purpose for which you are analyzing a case. For case briefs and class discussion, you probably will find that your teachers will move towards abstraction and generalization. For memos, you may tend to be more specific. In class, your teachers will probe to see how far they can move the case beyond its specific details. Even so, do not *write* an issue that goes so far beyond the facts that you lose the relationship with the case. Be as plain as you can about what happened, not vague, when you state an issue.

The Holding and the Rule

Your case brief should now progress from the question of law—the issue—to the court's answer to that question—the holding, and ultimately, the rule. Your teachers will differ about just how general a holding should be. Your sense of this will come only with experience. To start you on the path of experience, we will continue with the case of Jones pulling the tray out of Smith's hands.

One rather specific way to state a court's holding in that case would be to turn around the question that is the issue and make it a declarative sentence: "A person who pulls an object from another's hands in an insulting way is liable for a battery even though he did not touch the other person's body." This is a valid statement of a holding. It answers the question in terms of the facts of the case that raised the issue. It sends a signal to future possible litigants about what "the law" is concerning the tort consequences of indirect contacts. This holding is fairly specific to the facts and does not bite off more facts of future cases than it can chew. It does not invite unnecessary argument by being too broad. A broader holding, a more general one, might identify a larger category. For example, it might use the phrase "an object closely connected to the person of another" instead of "an object from another's hands in an insulting way." The "closely connected" terminology encompasses more events than contacts with items held in someone's hand. The most narrow holding would describe the object as a tray and repeat the defendant's insulting words.

The holding is not necessarily the same as a rule, for example, a definition of what a battery is. A holding is a statement of the court's decision in the case, in terms of the legal claim and the important facts of that case. It is the authoritative source of law from that case and it establishes a common law precedent. By comparison, a rule is a general statement of the law that prescribes, prohibits, or permits particular conduct. A common law rule usually results from a synthesis of several cases on the same issue. Not all the elements of the rule may be at issue in any one case. In the tray hypothetical, only the contact element of the definition of battery was at issue.

Most of your teachers, and many American judges, will approach a holding fairly broadly, and use it to look for relatively general principles governing the decision. Your teachers will engage you in this process by using hypotheticals. The holding of a case may then begin to look more like a rule of law. The holding in our *Smith v. Jones* hypothetical might form the basis for a relatively limited rule that a person may commit a battery by insultingly touching an object closely connected with the body of another.

There are at least two reasons why a court might wish to make a rule even broader. The court might want to indicate to people just how far they can go in venting their anger against others, at least with respect to certain legal consequences. Moreover, the court might want to signal attorneys dealing with cases that involve insulting contacts with things connected with others whether it would be prudent to litigate that behavior under the battery category. If those signals were clear, they would keep some cases out of court that might otherwise be litigated. They might also eventually reach beyond lawyers to the public, and thus help to keep the amount of antisocial conduct within tolerable limits.

Thus, perhaps we might want to make a somewhat more general statement of the "rule" about contact than our statement of the holding above. In an attempt to make you do that, teachers might present strings of hypothetical questions involving increasingly indirect contacts. Those hypotheticals might lead you to a more general statement of the contact element, for example, "A harmful or offensive act that results in an indirect contact with the body of another is a battery." This would make clear that the definition of battery does not limit itself to direct physical contacts, but also covers indirect ones. This definition would cover, for example, the case of someone who, while yelling vulgarities at the plaintiff, kicks a dog the plaintiff is holding on a leash. If we stated the rule in the broader way, no future defendant could argue, "I never touched the plaintiff's body and thus never directly offended his dignity in a way that justifies calling my act a battery."

A question that lies behind this formulation of a rule is whether the rule advances the interests of society. A proper answer to that question would require us to determine the basic rationale for the law of battery. We briefly discuss that very important inquiry at page 25-26 below, and give it fuller treatment later, especially in Chapters 9 and 10. That material will summarize some important tools of "policy" that help one to decide whether rules are good rules or bad rules. Our limited purpose in this section is to help you to state an operationally useful and fairly precise rule.

Applying the Rule

The court reaches its holding by applying the rule to the facts. In our *Smith v. Jones* hypothetical, the court will apply its definition of the contact element to the facts. It is useful, at least initially, to concentrate on doing this in syllogistic fashion. For those purposes, the rule is the major premise, the facts present the minor premise, and the application of the major premise to the minor premise leads to a conclusion.

The rule that the court used that is relevant to the case of the tray in the hand—the major premise—is that an intentional act that directly or indirectly causes an offensive contact with the person of another is a battery. Our facts—the minor premise—present a case in which one party intentionally caused an indirect contact by touching an object held by the other person although he did not directly touch the body of the other. To derive our conclusion, we apply our rule to the facts, and conclude that Jones committed a battery on Smith.

The Reasoning for the Decision

An important section in the traditional case brief includes the "reasoning," or rationale for a decision. Even simple rules depend for their persuasive power on reasons. As we will explain further in Chapters 9 and 10, American appellate courts tend to reason their way to legal conclusions at least partly on the basis of policy-based rationales. Those chapters will elaborate a little on some of the policies to which judges commonly refer in deciding difficult cases. However, even in your initial stage of learning to brief, you will begin to understand that competing policies may underlie such simple issues as whether a deliberate act that causes humiliation but does not result in a direct contact should be held to be a battery, with the overtones of wrongdoing that term carries.

In the case of Jones and Smith, Smith might argue that to label conduct like Jones's a battery will have good social results. Smith would contend that such liability for indirect contacts would deter people from violating the same dignitary interests clearly protected by the law of battery in the case of direct contacts.

By contrast, Jones would argue that the requirement of a direct contact serves as a rough kind of guarantee that serious consequences are likely to ensue to plaintiffs whose bodies are in fact directly touched, for otherwise people might be encouraged to bring frivolous litigation based on no more than insulting words and boorish behavior.   More generally, Jones would contend that society needs hard-edged and precise rules because they are easier for busy courts to administer than rules that lack sharply defined contours.   A court's decision for either party would reflect one of these competing rationales.

Law professors will urge students to dig out the policy arguments that underlie judicial decisions.   You may think, at least sometimes, that they push awfully far this idea of searching for the policy roots of rules, even simple rules.   Indeed, our illustrative use of policy in the simple case of the tray in the hand may be somewhat exaggerated. But you should get used to this policy-based form of analysis, because it is a useful tool in many legal situations.

Let your common sense remind you: somewhere there is a reason for every rule.   In some of the opinions you will read, the court may make you a gift; it may clearly state the reasons for its decision.   But if it did not, your professor will push you to think about a reason—a "rationale"—for the rule.

The Procedural Result

A good brief should make clear the procedural result of the case. It may be an affirmance of a dismissal. It may be the grant of a motion for a new trial. In the hypothetical we have been using about the tray in the hand, an appellate court would reverse the directed verdict that the trial court granted to the defendant. The applicable rule permits a plaintiff to claim a battery on the basis of contact with an object closely connected with the body, and the plaintiff offered evidence of such a contact. Thus, the appellate court will send the case back for a new trial under its definition of battery, which is broader than the one the trial court applied.

3

Precedent and How to Use It: Holding, Dictum and Rules

The Concept of Precedent

Courts put great stock in precedent. If a court has established a clear rule on a subject, it ordinarily will follow that rule. The governing Latin phrase is *stare decisis*, which means to adhere to decided cases. Occasionally, a court will overrule a prior decision, explicitly saying that the old decision no longer responds to social and economic realities, or perhaps even that the court was wrong the first time. Sometimes a court will implicitly overrule a prior decision. However, when there is a clear rule in a particular jurisdiction, for example, a state or a federal district, judges in that jurisdiction will follow it as the law. Precedent and the power to make rules for a particular jurisdiction are important concepts in our legal system.

Precedent plays an especially significant role for lower courts, because a lower court is bound by the decisions of higher courts in that jurisdiction on that issue. For example, a state intermediate appellate court will adhere to the decisions of that state's highest court on state law issues.[1]

Besides learning about the governing power of rules within particular jurisdictions, you will become familiar with the concept of

---

[1] One illustration of the very infrequent situation in which a lower court announces a contrary rule would be when a rule fixed by the highest court of a jurisdiction is very old, and most other jurisdictions have changed it. On a very few occasions an intermediate appellate court will change such a rule, and its decision will most likely be quickly appealed to the state's highest court for a binding determination.

persuasive authority from other jurisdictions. If one state or federal court has not ruled on a particular question, its judges will often consult the decisions of other states or federal courts that have dealt with that issue. Thus, decisions from those other courts may be persuasive on a question, although they do not have the mandatory authority of precedent from that jurisdiction. You may find, because your course work often treats cases and issues across jurisdictions, that you lose sight of the significance of the law of a specific jurisdiction. The law school process may encourage you to look at a general body of American law, although in actual practice, courts will require you to focus much more closely on the law of a particular jurisdiction.

Law school will expose you to differing perspectives about how courts view, and treat, cases. A rather cynical view is that judicial rulings depend on "what the judge ate for breakfast." A more sophisticated but also critical opinion suggests that judges are "result oriented"—they decide the outcome that they want to achieve on the basis of their personal philosophy, or their heart, or their gut, and then use intellectual hook or crook to achieve it.

We will not attempt here to argue with these views, which rest on some realistic insights about the human aspects of judging. However, it would be imprudent for you as a student to assume that judges do not take case law seriously, and it would be downright dangerous for you to act on that assumption when you are in practice. Moreover, depending on how cynical—or result-oriented—a particular professor is, it might not be wise for you to proceed, even in the classroom setting, on the belief that cases do not count.

Holding and Dictum

The idea of precedent is not one that courts apply mechanically. Indeed, judges possess several tools for defining the law within the framework of precedent, and these tools provide lawyers a lot of scope for creative argument. These include the concepts of holding, dictum, and rules.

Holding: Broad and Narrow Interpretations

We indicated above that a problem that frequently occupies courts is to decide how broadly to cast the holding in a case. In the narrowest sense, the holding represents a description of how the court answered the issue. The holding is the decision in a case consisting of the rule of law applied to the particular facts. Technically, only the holding is the binding law that emerges from that case.

The challenge for future litigants and courts is to define the holding in the context of their cases, when a court will look to precedents to determine the law that applies to the issue in that later case. In that situation, the court must decide how to interpret a precedent. Later courts can always restate the holding of a previous case as they interpret it. Many times a court will state the holding of the precedent broadly so that it is binding on the case at issue. The broader the statement, the more cases to which it will apply. If a court does not want to be bound by a precedent, it will describe the precedent narrowly so that it does not apply to the current case. Lawyers often call this technique "limiting the previous case to its facts."

For example, the law of gifts requires a delivery of the item being given. Suppose that in Case 1, the court held that an uncle's delivery to his niece of the key to his safe deposit box at a bank was effective to make a gift of the contents of the box. In Case 2, decided by the same court, an uncle buried gold coins in his backyard. He drew and gave to his niece a diagram showing where the coins were buried in order to make a gift of the coins to her. The court could interpret Case 1 as holding only that delivery of a key to a safe deposit box effects a gift of the contents of the box. However, the court could also interpret Case 1 as deciding that delivery of the means of access to an intended item of gift is sufficient delivery. This holding is broader and includes the facts of Case 2.

Now suppose that in both Cases 1 and 2, the uncles were ill and could not get to the bank to retrieve the contents of the box or dig up the gold in the backyard for presentation to the niece. In Case 3, however, a mother who is healthy gave her daughter the key to her office drawer, an act that the daughter claims made a gift of the stock certificates in the drawer. The court may decide that this is the same situation as the previous cases (access to the locked-up or hidden item of gift). However, by contrast, it might decide that an important fact in those cases was that the uncle could not retrieve the items in order to deliver them himself. If it adopted that view, the court would then add the fact of illness to its interpretation of the rule that came out of Cases 1 and 2, and conclude that because the mother could personally have gotten the stock certificate for delivery, her presentation of the drawer key was not a gift to her daughter of the certificates. (The difference in relationship between the parties—uncle and niece and mother and daughter—should be irrelevant; that is, it should make no difference to the outcome.)

Dicta

Language in a precedent case that is not necessary for its decision is not binding and is called dicta (the singular is dictum). One way to describe dicta is as pronouncements in which a court goes beyond the bounds of the kind of statement that is necessary to produce the decision that governs a particular case. Law-trained people make a rather sharp distinction between holding and dicta. Since dicta are non-authoritative statements in a court's decision, courts in future cases are free to disregard them. However, judges frequently use dicta for various reasons. For example, they may discern other legal problems on the horizon that are analogous to the one in the case before them, and for the purpose of controlling their dockets they may want to send signals to lawyers and litigants about the sorts of cases they will entertain and those that they will reject.

Suppose, for example, that a court with a strong "free speech" majority has before it a prosecution for statements that offended a particular group, such as members of a religion. The court decides that to allow prosecution for such remarks would violate the First Amendment. But a majority of the justices, feeling as strongly as they do about liberating all kinds of speech, decide that they want to send prosecutors a more general message. Their opinion declares, "The First Amendment is so broad that its prohibition on government interference with speech applies across the board to offensive and even repulsive uses of language, including not only speech that is hateful to particular groups but even pornography."

The court's declaration about pornography would be dictum, for it is not in any way necessary to decide the case at issue, which deals only with "hate speech." It represents the appellate court's effort to advise lawyers, potential litigants—and lower courts—about its views on a general set of legal issues related to free speech. Such broad statements can provide useful signals for future litigation, although many lawyers would prefer that courts limit their inclinations to issue dicta and would say that judges should try to stick to the case at hand.

An example of a more difficult holding/dictum question would be this: The case before a court deals with a hateful anti-gay statement, and the court concludes that it would violate the First Amendment to prosecute the maker of the statement. But instead of confining itself to the issue of anti-gay declarations, the court says, "It is unconstitutional to regulate speech that offends any societal group—homosexuals, racial minorities and religious groups—because the First Amendment informs us that the antidote for bad speech is good speech and, in any event, more speech." This judicial statement presents a closer question than the reference to pornography discussed above, because this one deals only with hate speech, although it refers to groups other than gays. Yet, many people would say that the reference to groups other than gays is dictum.

There is thus room for a serious difference of opinion on this issue of holding/dictum, and we do not have to resolve that question here. Rather, our point is simply that you should recognize that the issue exists. The practical problem is how a court in that jurisdiction should view the broader statement, embracing several groups, when it is considering a future case involving hate speech directed against a group other than gays, for example, a racial minority. The court in the later case might say that the broader statement was the "holding" of the earlier case, and thus binding on its own decision, or it might say that it is not bound by the broader statement in the earlier case because it was dictum.

The Tension Between Broad and Narrow Rules

We have suggested that courts face a tension between resolving a single dispute and fashioning a broader "rule of law." There are competing truths here. Courts exist to resolve disputes, individual controversies that arise between parties who are in court at particular times. But courts, especially appellate courts, also have a lawgiving—even lawmaking—function. In connection with that function, they are supposed to provide some explanation to the community about why they have decided for Smith and not for Jones. The statement of a rule contributes to that explanation. The rule tells the community the major premise from which the court derived its particularized conclusion—that is, its decision.

This technique of rulemaking helps to bring efficiency to the administration of justice. If the court states a relatively broad rule in one case, and does so effectively, it may avoid five more disputes that might otherwise come to it. This is because the rule will advise claimants' lawyers, "Don't bother—here's the rule, and it tells you that your case won't have a chance," or, it will tell defendants' attorneys, "You had better settle this one without fighting it; it's a clear loser."

There are opposing arguments, however. If a court states a rule too broadly, it will invite a lot of wrangling in the future about what it meant. It will create more need for interpretation, and resultant uncertainty, than if it stuck to a relatively narrow rule that is just enough to decide the case before it. People who take this position concerning a particular judicial opinion will emphasize the constraining idea that courts exist to resolve disputes. They will say something to this effect: "Instead of trying to set out broad rules for future disputes—which is a legislative task rather than a judicial one—judges should confine themselves to solving the problem before them. If other cases are going to arise that are analogous to the instant case (the one before the court) it will be time enough to deal with them when they come. When they do appear, the court can then formulate a concrete rule that solves them."

Stability, Room for Argument, and the Psychology of Law Study

The subject of holding and dictum leads to a practical point that will trouble many students, but is one with which you should get comfortable. This is simply that law is always subject to argument. You will rarely be working with unassailable ideas. There are few clear "yes's" or "no's" in law school.

People complain that lawyers are argumentative. That is partly in the nature of law. It is true, of course, that law is a stabilizing force in our society. There are thousands of "rules" that we accept as relatively fixed governing standards for the way we live. But the law also is a vital and growing thing, and it deals constantly with specific facts. That means that on any legal subject that is worth discussion—which means the kinds of questions that often get presented in law school courses—there will be a lot of room for disagreement, even disagreement over what a prior decision means.

This is not welcome news to many law students, who want the security of a well-defined rule. A subject that engenders constant argument introduces uncertainty into your life, and you probably will find unsettling the fact that the law is full of uncertainties. You should try to get used to this feature of law study, however. At least, you may take some comfort from the fact that all your classmates face the same uncertainties. Moreover, you should understand that this mode of operation represents practical training. Lawyers, particularly lawyers dealing with litigation or efforts to avoid litigation, always have to be thinking about what an opponent will say, for example, how the opponent will interpret precedents or statutory language. The more practice you get in reflexively considering possible arguments against the position you represent, the more secure you will feel with this technique.

Because of the disputatious character of law, you should not be surprised to find that matters of great controversy—the sort of questions that get to appellate courts and into law school coursebooks—often will inspire judges on the same court to write separate opinions. Judges who have outright disagreements with a decision may write dissenting opinions. Others, who agree with the outcome of a decision but differ on matters of reasoning or breadth of holding, may write another kind of separate opinion (often called a concurrence) that explains their points of view. The existence of these judicial disagreements, which will become second nature to you, simply underlines that you should not be surprised to find argument about what the correct rule is or should be.

A study tip that grows from this point is that when you find a dissenting or concurring opinion in a coursebook, you should pay particular attention to the clash of ideas between that opinion and the majority opinion. Coursebook editors are highly selective about the cases they pick and the portions of opinions they choose to print. If they present a dissenting or concurring opinion in a book, they are trying to develop an important point of controversy. They may be signaling, for example, that you should consider whether the separate opinion is better reasoned and more persuasive than that of the majority.

It may be helpful to conclude with a point of personal psychology. The argumentative style of law school may spill over into your personal life. You may find yourself trying to score adversary points with a non-lawyer spouse, roommate, or parent. After a while, you will understand, consciously, that this is just part of lawyers' play. It would be useful if you become aware of this tendency early. You might even want to show this section to your spouse, or friend, or parent, to help him or her understand.

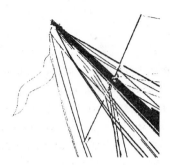

4

Expanding On Procedure

This chapter presents a brief overview of the procedural framework that courts apply to civil disputes—the system of "civil procedure." Most law schools will introduce you to this subject primarily through the Federal Rules of Civil Procedure, a comprehensive code that embodies the basic principles of the subject. Besides actually governing procedure in all federal litigation, the Federal Rules provide a nice model for classroom discussion of basic procedural principles. Each state has its own separate set of rules—some of which follow the Federal Rules—that govern procedure in civil disputes. Some instructors may employ state procedural codes in their classes. This chapter, using terminology that is fairly basic to both federal and state procedural systems, approaches the subject primarily through the prism of the motions that parties most often make at crucial stages of litigation, although none of these motions is mandatory. When you read a case and brief it, it usually is important to note its procedural history, specifying, for example, any motion on which the case was decided.

The Complaint

Civil litigation usually begins when the plaintiff (or claimant) files a document called a complaint. The complaint must announce the jurisdictional basis for the court to take the case and identify the plaintiff's grievance. There is theoretical dispute, and there are differences among jurisdictions, about just how specific the complaint must be. Subject to the requirement that in some cases, the plaintiff must swear to certain kinds of material, an important controversy turns on whether the complaint should be quite precise about the *facts* on which the plaintiff is relying or whether it may allege just enough to put the defendant on *notice* of what the plaintiff will later try to prove. This dispute involves policy issues concerning both the fairness and the economics of the litigation process: On the one hand, on the plaintiff's initial trip to the courtroom, how far do we want to push her into the business of specifying evidence, especially when critical evidence may be within the control of the defendant? On the other hand, is it fair to the defendant to allow a relatively vague complaint that forces him at an early stage to expend resources to defend against a relatively unspecified grievance?

Whether a jurisdiction requires fact or notice pleading, complaints offer *allegations, not proof.* The court considers a complaint on the assumption that the plaintiff will be able to prove what she alleges, but the complaint itself consists only of assertions.

At the least, the complaint should disclose a theory of liability or other basis in law for the lawsuit. To borrow an example from Chapter 2, a plaintiff might contend that someone committed a battery on him by pulling a tray out of his hand while yelling insults. One way to present that theory would be simply to allege the fact that the defendant yanked the tray away in a nasty way. It is helpful, however—even necessary—to specify a particular legal doctrine: that of battery. This would frame the theory that the defendant acted intentionally to bring about a harmful or offensive contact. The issue of whether it is a battery for someone to make contact with an object closely connected to the plaintiff, rather than making direct contact with the plaintiff's body, would present a question of law for the court. That issue could be resolved on one of the procedural motions discussed below.

The Motion to Dismiss

The first major checkpoint after the filing of a complaint appears with the defendant's opportunity to file a motion to dismiss; a synonym, still used in some states, is a "demurrer." The motion to dismiss is just what its name explains. The defendant asks the court to dismiss the plaintiff's complaint—to say that the lawsuit is at an end because the complaint is legally deficient. Initially, the theory behind this motion is hard for many students to grasp. You may have to wrestle with a substantial number of cases before the concept begins to take hold. A threshold element of a motion to dismiss is that it allows the court to assume, for the purposes of argument, that the plaintiff can prove all the facts that she alleges in her complaint. Given that assumption, the motion to dismiss asks, "So what?" In essence, the defendant says to the plaintiff, "Even if you can prove all your allegations, there is no legal rule to support your claim."

The motion to dismiss, then, challenges the plaintiff to show that there is law to support the theory of her complaint. It thus presents a "question of law." If the plaintiff cannot invoke a legal rule that supports her action, the court will dismiss the complaint and the suit will end there unless the plaintiff appeals.

Let us now return to our hypothetical case about the tray. The definition of the tort of battery requires the plaintiff to show that the defendant intentionally committed a harmful or offensive touching "with the person of another." In our hypothetical, the plaintiff alleged that the defendant intentionally touched a tray he was carrying, but did not claim that the defendant touched his body. Since the traditional definition of battery requires a touching of the person of another, the defendant would move to dismiss, and the court would have to decide whether the defendant's contact with a tray held by another would fall within that definition. Some courts would dismiss the case, reasoning that as a matter of law—the law of battery—there was no battery because the defendant did not make contact with the body of the plaintiff. Other courts would deny the motion to dismiss, reasoning that contact with an object closely connected with someone falls within the practical meaning of the phrase "with the person of another." We make two points here: (1) a motion to dismiss requires the court to decide whether on *assumed facts*, there is a legal rule on which the plaintiff may rely; (2) Different courts may respond in opposite ways to questions of law.

This relatively simple illustration highlights the distinction between allegations and proof. If a court decided that for the purposes of the law of battery, nastily touching the tray would be enough like touching the plaintiff's body to be a contact with "the person of another," then there might be a dispute about whether the defendant offensively touched the tray. If there was such a controversy, it would present a *question of fact* for the judge or the jury to decide. But at the motion to dismiss stage, the court does not concern itself with the factual truth of the plaintiff's allegations. Indeed, if the court denies the defendant's motion to dismiss, it does not decide at that point that the defendant is, or is not, liable to the plaintiff. Making the assumption that the plaintiff's allegations are true only for purposes of the motion, the court considers only whether there is a rule of law that would support recovery if the plaintiff proves those allegations at trial.

Alternatively to filing a motion to dismiss, or, if the motion to dismiss is unsuccessful, the defendant must file an answer to the complaint. This pleading may take several forms. The defendant may deny the plaintiff's allegations, or may allege facts that would refute the facts pleaded by the plaintiff. The focus of the answer is on the facts alleged by the plaintiff, rather than the legal theory presented in the complaint.

Motion for Summary Judgment

As litigation progresses, the parties will be collecting information and evidence about the case, through what is called the "discovery" process. They may, for example, collect facts through depositions, which are oral examinations of parties or witnesses under oath, and interrogatories, which are questions propounded by counsel in writing to the other party.

The next principal checkpoint in litigation is the motion for summary judgment. Either party may make this motion. A party who moves for summary judgment asks the court to decide the case without a trial. She contends that she is entitled to judgment on a combination of law and facts, but those facts will not include testimony by live witnesses at trial who are subject to cross-examination. Rather, summary judgment facts will be limited, typically, to documentary evidence, such as depositions or interrogatories. It also would include affidavits of people who might later testify at a trial if it is held, as well as contracts, property deeds, or letters.

The party seeking summary judgment would argue that, given the applicable legal rule and the facts exhibited by the documents, a reasonable court would be compelled to rule in its favor. The effect of a summary judgment is to dispose of a case without a trial. For the court to hold that way, there must be a rule that is capable of concrete application to documentary evidence, although the rule may be a rather general one. Moreover, the "fact" evidence presented by the maker of the motion for summary judgment must be specific and convincing enough to persuade the court that a trial would add no facts necessary for decision. A court may grant summary judgment only if there is no dispute about any material facts, and it is important to understand that the court cannot make credibility judgments at the summary judgment stage.

An example would be a case in which a plaintiff claimed that a drug caused injury to her, but offered no expert testimony on causation. The defendant, by contrast, presented the affidavits of five qualified scientists who declared that two dozen studies on the clinical effects of the drug had demonstrated no statistical association between use of the product and the kind of injury the plaintiff suffered. One applicable rule of law would be a rule that a plaintiff in a personal injury case must show that it is more probable than not that the defendant's conduct or product caused the plaintiff's injury. Since all of the evidence before the court indicated that the probabilities were that the product at issue did not cause that injury, the court presumably would grant summary judgment for the defendant. The reason would be that under the law—that is, the requirement that personal injury plaintiffs show a probability of causation—the defendant's uncontradicted factual evidence that there was no such probability requires the conclusion that there is no reasonable basis to hold for the plaintiff. By contrast, if the parties' documents included conflicting evidence on causation, then the court would deny the motion and require a trial on the facts.

The Motion for Directed Verdict (Motion For Judgment as a Matter of Law)

If a case goes to trial, then after the presentation of evidence, either party may make what historically has been called a motion for directed verdict. Under a 1991 amendment to Rule 50(a) of the Federal Rules of Civil Procedure, this motion has now been translated into the term motion for judgment as a matter of law. That terminology now governs all federal court decisions, although many states still preserve the "directed verdict" label, as do the pre-1991 federal cases. For the sake of convenience, we will use the term "motion for directed verdict" to describe this motion, which the defendant typically will initially make after the plaintiff presents his evidence, and the plaintiff will make at the close of all the evidence.

There is a costly jump between the stage of the pre-trial motions to dismiss and for summary judgment, on the one hand, and the motion for directed verdict on the other hand. The jump occurs because in the interim, a trial has begun, an event that involves a steep rise in expense. The judge must spend his or her time presiding over the trial, at the cost of dealing with other matters on the court calendar. The trial ties up other officials, jurors if there is a jury trial, and a courtroom. Those are the social expenses. The costs to parties themselves will also escalate, with attorneys' fees being a substantial part of the toll.

The important point for our present purposes—a brief explanation of the motion for a directed verdict—is that a trial involves witnesses. It goes beyond not only the motion to dismiss, which involves arguments only about law, but also beyond the summary judgment stage, where the court considers documents along with the law.

When there are live witnesses, the judge and the jury must both consider the demeanor of witnesses and make judgments about their credibility. In addition, they must weigh for its persuasiveness the testimony of witnesses who often will be in open conflict, including conflict about how an event occurred.

The motion for directed verdict represents an effort by the maker of the motion to persuade the court that in light of the applicable law, and the facts that have been developed by the time the motion is offered, the party seeking the directed verdict *must* win. The theory is that given the facts presented at trial that are most favorable to the party who did not make the directed verdict motion (the "nonmoving party"), that party could not succeed under the law. This is analogous to both the motion to dismiss and the motion for summary judgment in this sense: The party making the motion for directed verdict in effect tells the court that she is willing to concede, for the sake of argument, the facts that the other party claims to have proved. Even so, the "moving party" insists, what the nonmoving party proved is not enough to make a case under the law. We have said this several different ways in order to give you a variety of opportunities to understand the function of the motion for directed verdict. However, the only way you will truly grasp the point is to read a lot of cases in which that motion is crucial.

Here is an exaggerated example involving an automobile accident. Cars driven by Mr. A and Ms. B collide. Mr. A suffers injuries and sues Ms. B for negligence. Mr. A has no recollection of the accident. Ms. B and three eyewitnesses testify that the light was green in Ms. B's favor and two other eyewitnesses testify that the light was red against Mr. A. Ms. B moves for a directed verdict. Given a legal rule that running a red light is a form of negligence that will bar recovery for injuries by a driver who does that, the court would grant Ms. B's motion. In the light of the evidence, as well as the legal rule, no reasonable person could find in favor of Mr. A, the nonmoving party.

Motion for Judgment Notwithstanding the Verdict (Judgment N.O.V.) (Renewed Motion for Judgment as a Matter of Law)

The motions we have discussed to this point occur either at the preliminary stages of litigation or during the trial. After a trial is over and the fact finder reaches a verdict, the losing party usually will make two motions. The first is what historically has been called the motion for judgment notwithstanding the verdict (judgment n.o.v.). Rule 50(b) of the Federal Rules of Civil Procedure now calls this post-trial motion a renewed motion for judgment as a matter of law. For convenience, we refer to it as a motion for judgment n.o.v.

In making this motion, the losing party in effect offers the court an opportunity to correct what the losing party perceives as a misjudgment during the trial. Your procedure teacher will discuss many technical refinements concerning this motion, but a very simplified way to look at it is to view it like an after-trial repetition of the motion for directed verdict. In moving for judgment n.o.v., the losing party often will in effect be urging that the trial judge made a mistake in not granting a motion for directed verdict during the trial. The maker of the motion—who at the moment has lost the trial judgment—contends that under the law, and the best version of the facts from the prevailing party's point of view, the trial judgment was wrong and that indeed no reasonable person could have held for the prevailing party. "Please reconsider what you did on the directed verdict now that you have the hindsight of the entire trial—and perhaps a less hurried look at the law." That is what the maker of a motion for judgment n.o.v. respectfully tells the judge.

Let us briefly tie together the last several sections. When a court grants any of the motions discussed immediately above—(1) to dismiss (2) for summary judgment (3) for a directed verdict (judgment as a matter of law) (4) judgment n.o.v. (judgment as a matter of law after trial)—it is saying that reasonable persons could not disagree about the outcome. In the case of the motion to dismiss, it makes its ruling entirely on the law. In the case of the motion for summary judgment, it considers both law and documentary evidence.

Finally, in the case of the motions for directed verdict and judgment n.o.v., it takes into account both the law and the facts as they have been developed in a trial. In each instance, a court that grants one of these motions concludes that the nonmoving party has no case under the law.

Motion for New Trial

The motion for a new trial represents the other major opportunity for the losing party to convince the trial judge, or an appellate court, to reverse the results of a trial. For our present simplified purposes, this is a catch-all motion that asks the court to declare that there was some kind of legal error in the trial.

One frequent reason for seeking a new trial is that the court made an erroneous statement of law in its instructions to the jury. A common error is a misstatement of an applicable legal rule. Consider, for example, a situation in which the law requires that in order to convict a defendant of a certain crime, the prosecution must show that the defendant behaved "purposefully." Despite that rule, a court instructs the jury that it can convict if the defendant behaved "reck-lessly," a lesser requirement that is not as difficult to prove. If the jury brings in a verdict of guilty, the defendant could move for a new trial on grounds that the instruction misstated the law.

Another reason for seeking a new trial relates to the manner in which the trial was held, including the conduct of the lawyers. One example would be a criminal case with high emotional content in the community, in which the defendant claims that he or she could not get a fair trial in the county where the trial was held. In ruling on a motion for a new trial, the court would have to decide whether the psychological environment of the proceedings rendered the trial unfair.

A more everyday illustration would be a request for a new trial on the grounds that the court erred in a ruling on the evidence. For example, a losing party might claim that the court admitted the testimony of an unqualified witness. Or, by contrast, that party might argue that the court improperly decided that a witness was unqualified when it should have allowed that person to testify. In that case, the losing party would contend that the evidence that was excluded would have made a difference in her favor.

5

Roles of Judge and Jury; Facts and Law

Our outline of main topics in procedure leads directly to a brief introduction to two related subjects: the way the legal system divides litigation tasks between judges and juries, and the distinction between questions of "fact" and questions of "law." As is so with most important legal topics, most students will fully grasp these ideas only after exposure to many cases.

Judges Rule on the Law

A fundamental point is that judges, not juries, rule on the law. This makes good sense. Judges have legal educations. They, or their clerks, know how to use a law library. To take just one example, if the question arises as to whether a particular crime requires proof that the defendant had a purpose to injure the victim or whether the prosecution can succeed by showing only that the defendant acted recklessly in injuring the victim, it is the judge who must decide the question. This is a question of law, to be answered by professionals consulting statutes or judicial decisions, or deciding the question for the first time. It is not an issue for jury determination.

Juries Decide Facts

A second fundamental principle is that jurors, where there is a jury, decide facts. (When a trial is to a judge alone ("a bench trial") the judge acts as a "fact finder" as well as ruling on the law.) Sometimes the question of fact (or "fact issue") is a simple one. Did A hit B? Did C drive through the intersection while the light was red? Sometimes it is more subtle: Did A purposely hit B? It may have even more nuances: Was A substantially certain that he would cause a harmful or offensive contact to B? With reference to any question of fact, even relatively subtle ones, the practical premise is that the jury is making a decision, based on the evidence at the trial, with respect to what happened or what exists. That determination, it should be noted, does not necessarily dispose of "the facts"; jury determinations of fact are subject to judicial review. A court may decide, on combing through the evidence, that a jury could not reasonably have found "the facts" as it did.

Distinguishing Issues of Law and Fact

Sometimes one has to work at telling the difference between a question of fact and one of law. One of us understood the distinction a little better during a ride on a state highway lined with signs warning about statutes that impose fines for littering. She wondered whether she would be guilty of littering if she threw out the car window the core of the apple she had just finished eating. Is an apple core "litter" if it is biodegradable and is nourishing to the grass on the shoulder? The question of who threw the core out the window would be a question of fact. The question of whether an apple core is litter is a question of law. The judge must use her professional training in statutory interpretation to analyze the term "litter" to decide whether that term includes biodegradable objects.

Areas of Uncertainty

When a judge reviews a jury's verdict on the facts, she measures that verdict against a relatively objective standard concerning events as they took place or a state of the world that can be observed or verified.[1] The questions of what is objective and what is measurable frequently will lead decisionmakers into areas of uncertainty. If the issue is whether A had a purpose to hit B, or made contact with B only recklessly and not purposefully, then we are no longer in territory where we can ask, with relative certainty, whether the light was red.

However, as courts tend to classify these issues, we are still in an area where judges ordinarily leave the question to the jury. That happens frequently in cases involving suits for allegedly negligent conduct. A judge will ask a jury whether a defendant acted "unreasonably" in not clearing his walk of ice and snow. Purists might desire a quantitative standard for such questions—one must use so many tablespoons of salt on so many square feet of ice—but common sense tells us that, in a lot of cases of that sort, there is no numerical test. Despite the lack of a scientific gauge, courts often say that this kind of issue presents a "question of fact" for the jury about whether the defendant behaved "reasonably."

Still, there will come a time when a court will say that a jury acted unreasonably in deciding a question of "fact," and will reverse the jury's verdict for that reason. Let us say that in a busy supermarket, a customer reaching for something on a shelf knocks over a bottle of cooking oil that breaks and spills. The next person coming up the aisle slips on the oil within the next minute and a half. A sympathetic jury might say that the market was "unreasonable" in not cleaning up the oil and hold the store negligent in a suit by the person who slipped. But a judge might grant judgment n.o.v. to the store on the ground that it would be unreasonable to require anyone to clean up a spill of liquid in a supermarket aisle within 90 seconds.

One way to ease the tensions created by sharp distinctions between "law" and "fact" is to speak of "mixed questions of law and fact." Some of your teachers will take you through the complexities of these concepts, and you will learn to deal with these ideas reflexively after you read a lot of cases. For now, it is worth underlining a few simplified ideas: judges rule on the law, juries (or judges acting as fact finders) find facts, and sometimes judges control "unreasonable"

---

[1] Students with training in such subjects as philosophy will recognize the oversimplified character of this definition, but we believe it will be of practical help.

jury verdicts by saying that, under the law, no one reasonably could have found the "facts" the way the jury did.

6

Legal Reasoning

This chapter discusses several types of thought processes typical to lawyers' work. Some of these logical processes will be familiar to you from your previous academic work as well as from your prior experiences in life.

Inductive Reasoning

Lawyers engage in reasoning that is sometimes inductive—that is, from the particular to the general—and sometimes deductive—working from the general to the particular—and they go back and forth between these techniques.

Inductive reasoning, which is a fair amount of the thinking that lawyers do, consists of reasoning up from a chain of particular cases to a general rule. Assume that over time, the courts of one state decide a series of three cases in which one person tells a second person that the first person is willing to pay a named sum of money for a certain kind of activity or accomplishment. It might be mowing the first person's lawn, or giving information that leads to the apprehension of a criminal, or shooting a hole-in-one in golf. In each of these cases, a third person who did not previously hear about the first person's willingness to pay for the designated accomplishment actually achieves that result. In the first of these cases, the third person mows the first person's lawn; in the second case, the third person produces information that helps catch a robber; in the third case, the third person shoots a hole-in-one. In each case, the third person hears later about the first person's offer, and asks that the first person pay for what he has done. In each case, the first person rebuffs the request for payment and the third person brings a contract action. Although not articulating a crisp rule that guides its decisions in the first two cases, and describing their holdings very narrowly, the court rejects the third person's suit for the named sum in those cases. By the time it decides the third case, however, the court begins to perceive a general rule that governs all three cases. In rejecting the claim of the person who shot the hole-in-one, it articulates that rule as being that no one may recover for performance in response to an offer unless he knew of the offer before performance.

We can test out that rule with a fourth case that comes along later. In this case, the third person knew before he performed a task—let us say washing the defendant's windows—about the defendant's statement to another person that he would pay someone to wash his house windows. This plaintiff will win his suit for payment, because he knew about the offer before he performed the requested task even though the offer was not made to him.

This kind of development of a legal rule represents a form of induction—using several specific holdings to derive a more general rule. You may discern that besides being a technique of "legal reasoning," this is one way that people learn and run their lives generally. People learn by creating categories of information. They accumulate a group of specific experiences, and they generalize from them to fashion standards for guiding their responses to new situations.

This inductive mode of thought also captures an important feature of what many lawyers think of as "the genius of the common law"—that is, judge-made law. The common law proceeds by increments, building precedent on precedent. It then establishes general rules and, as new cases arise, broadens or narrows those rules or creates exceptions to them. In our basic example, the court synthesized three cases; it put them together to formulate the rule that governed them.

The conclusions you reach by inductive reasoning are not necessarily true, or valid in the sense used in formal logic. The cases you use as evidence to support your conclusion (your general rule) don't necessarily compel that conclusion. Consider the examples in Chapter 3, at pages 29-30, about delivery of a key to a safe deposit box and of a map of buried gold. In that chapter, we synthesized a rule from the two cases that delivery of the means of access to property is effective delivery for purposes of making a gift of that property. We also said there that the relationship between the donor (the person who gives the gift) and the recipient (the donee) as uncle and nephew, or mother and daughter, was not relevant to the rule, although the fact that the donor was ill and could not retrieve the property himself was relevant. We made these conclusions based on our judgment about the cases and that area of the law; those judgments may not be accurate, and later cases may show that they are not accurate.

Induction, however, is a matter of probabilities, not certainty. We were saying that in our judgment it is very likely that the relationship between the parties was not relevant to the rule we formulated. However, by contrast with our prediction of probabilities—which is a personal forecast, based on inductive reasoning from precedent—when the highest court in a jurisdiction arrives at the same conclusion, it is the law. Thus, if a state supreme court concluded that delivery of the means of access to property is effective delivery if the donor is ill and cannot retrieve the property, and does not distinguish by the relationship between donor and donee, then the court has announced a rule that is certain for purposes of the law of that jurisdiction, until the court overrules it or qualifies it at some later date. That rule will then be applied deductively (see pages 54-56 below).

Synthesizing Cases

The ability to synthesize cases is an important tool in your kit of legal skills. Legal synthesis involves multiple precedents—at least two, and sometimes many more. When you synthesize cases, you seek to put together two or more precedents involving a fairly specific topic. Typically, these decisions will not have announced really distinct principles; or perhaps the principles they do articulate are so narrow that they cover only the case that was then before the court. The synthesizer will seek to use those precedents to establish a new, relatively comprehensive principle that embraces the prior cases as well as the case at issue.

An example comes from the subject of torts. Over a period of years, courts began to impose liability on people who had mishandled dead bodies, in suits brought by relatives of the dead person. In apparently very separate developments, courts also began to impose liability on bill collectors for deliberately harassing behavior, in suits by vexed debtors. Finally, in a third group of seemingly unrelated cases, some courts began to give recovery to persons who complained of what today would be called sexual harassment, although that term was not initially used.

A leading torts scholar *synthesized* these lines of cases by finding certain common threads among them. He saw those threads as including three specific elements: (1) the defendant had behaved intentionally to (2) cause the plaintiff severe emotional distress (3) and the defendant's conduct was so reprehensible—"outrageous"—as to be an offense against decency. He brought together this synthesis of seemingly unlike cases under the heading of a new tort action, the doctrine now called "intentional infliction of emotional distress."[1]

Besides synthesizing cases to form a rule that defines a claim, judges and lawyers also synthesize facts in an effort to identify the types of factors that courts consider persuasive as proving or disproving claims. For example, if a person (the testator) is known to have executed a will, but the will cannot be found after the testator dies, the court must decide whether the testator intentionally revoked the will (by burning it, for example) or instead, inadvertently lost the will. Drawing on several cases, you might identify facts that were important to the decisions in those cases, which you then could group into categories. One category of facts may concern the identity of the person who looked for the will; another category may include evidence about whether the testator had reasons to want to revoke the

---

[1] William L. Prosser, Intentional Infliction of Mental Suffering: A New Tort, 37 Mich. L. Rev. 874 (1939).

will or to make changes; yet another may involve the security of the location at which the testator kept the will. When you see similarities among sets of facts you can fashion these categories, and can relate the categories to the claims being litigated. For example, if the person who searched for the will would benefit by the will not being found, because that person was not named in the will, then the searcher may have had a motive to destroy the will and one might conclude that the testator did not lose or revoke the will.

It will take you some time, and a fair amount of practice, to grasp the idea of legal synthesis. One purpose of this section is simply to alert you to the idea that individual cases do not exist in a historical vacuum. It follows that sometimes there are ways that one can put together lines of cases to derive a new principle. Of course, the job of the lawyer who opposes the new principle is to show that the cases can be distinguished—that they are not as much alike (or similar, or analogous) as the proponent of the synthesis claims that they are.

Exceptions to Rules (or New Rules)

As the common law grows by synthesis—the development of rules from a series of cases—it begins to develop exceptions to rules to meet new situations. Assume that over a period of time, a court develops the rule that killing another human being is murder. Soon, however, the court becomes troubled by the injustice of applying that rule to a case in which someone kills another in order to protect her own life. The court thus develops an exception to the rule that killing another human being is murder. The exception is, "unless the killing is done in self-defense."

As more cases come along, and the law expands, an exception may become so complex that it becomes a rule—or a set of rules—in itself. Thus, to continue our criminal law illustration, we may speak of "the self-defense rules"—a group of rules that evolve in response to a series of cases that present variations on the general situation of killing for self-protection. One of those rules, which may vary among jurisdictions, requires a person to retreat before using deadly force in self-defense, at least if she may retreat safely. Still another rule gives a person the privilege to use deadly force in self-defense, without the need to retreat, if the person is in her own home.

The main point to remember is that many rules have exceptions, and that exceptions sometimes become significant enough that they become new sets of rules in themselves.

Applying General Rules: Deduction

By contrast with the inductive method that formulates general rules from concrete cases, the technique of deductive reasoning applies general ru'es to particular facts, or, as lawyers say, applies the law to the facts. Courts and lawyers use this type of reasoning when general rules already have been fashioned, by statute or by previous judicial decision (that is, by induction).

A common law illustration begins with the procedural requirement that a court must grant a directed verdict when the evidence is such that reasonable persons could not differ on the outcome. Let us say that there is a substantive rule of state tort law, fashioned from precedents, that says that one cannot establish a medical malpractice case without expert testimony that a doctor was negligent. The plaintiff presents facts from which many lay persons would deduce that a doctor behaved negligently, but does not offer expert testimony. Thus, the plaintiff has not met the requirements of the substantive rule. Since the governing procedural rule on directed verdicts declares that a plaintiff cannot get to the jury unless reasonable persons could differ on the outcome, the court must direct a verdict for the defendant. Given a substantive rule that requires expert testimony to support a malpractice case, jurors could not reasonably find for a plaintiff who did not present expert testimony.

Deductive reasoning is syllogistic in its pattern. In legal applications, it starts from a general rule (a major premise—the rule requiring expert testimony). It focuses on a particular set of facts (the minor premise—the plaintiff's failure to present expert testimony). Then it moves to a conclusion (a directed verdict because there was no expert testimony). In formal logic, the conclusion is compelled by the premises. Lawyers who argue for a particular result try to fit the governing rule and its application to the facts of a case into this syllogistic pattern to compel a judgment for their clients.

A statutory example of deductive reasoning applies a state statute that requires a will to be signed by two witnesses in order to be valid. This requirement of two witnesses is the major premise. The minor premise for our purposes is the fact, offered by a litigant contesting the will, that a disputed will was signed by one witness. Applying the statutory rule (major premise—requirement of two witnesses) to the particular case (minor premise—only one witness signed the will), we must conclude that the will is not valid.

However, few issues will be that simple. You should understand that deduction as we illustrate it here supplies only a pattern for legal analysis. The simplicity of that pattern may hide the difficult analytical work that precedes its articulation. Sometimes the difficulty lies in supplying the major premise, that is, the accepted rule, because the issue has not yet been decided in that jurisdiction. Then the lawyer or the court must first work inductively to determine the rule in that jurisdiction. Sometimes the rule is not clear, for example, when statutory language can be interpreted in more than one way. Then the lawyer or the court must analyze the statute and interpret its language to derive the major premise.

Often the difficulty lies in formulating the minor premise. Consider, for example, a statute that requires witnesses to a will to "sign in the presence of the testator." Ask yourself: Do witnesses sign in the testator's "presence" if the testator is inside her office, looking out through a window, and the witnesses are in her direct view, signing the will while leaning on the hood of a car parked directly across from the window? Or does "presence" require that the parties all be in the same room, or all be standing together so that they see each other writing? There will not likely be a precedent with the exact facts of the hypothetical of the "witnesses" leaning on the car, and it is probable that the legislature did not provide a definition of "presence." Thus, in order to analyze this issue, and to supply the minor premise concerning whether the witnesses signed in the testator's presence, you will have to reason by analogy to similar cases involving the statutory term "sign in the presence of the testator." In a sense, you also have to reason inductively again in order to determine what "presence" means. The next section provides a brief introduction to reasoning by analogy.

Reasoning By Analogy

A powerful tool for law work, one almost instinctively used by people with legal training, is reasoning by analogy. A simplified introduction to this form of reasoning in the legal context lies in the phrase, "This case is like that case," a statement that implies that the two cases should be treated the same. In "that" case, facts 1, 2, and 3 were present and the plaintiff won. In "this" case, facts 1, 2, and 3 are also present, and the plaintiff should win. People use this form of reasoning for many purposes, not just legal ones, especially when they analyze a new problem. To analyze a new problem, one looks for existing solutions to problems of the same kind to see how those who solved the prior problems examined them. We have been using examples of reasoning by analogy throughout this book because it is the essence of a lawyer's work.

Besides helping you to identify similarities in cases, reasoning by analogy also will aid you to analyze differences between and among cases. As you go through law school, it will become second nature to you to find such distinctions. You may become argumentative to the point that you will pick on small variations between cases and say that they make a difference. That is a developed ability that is important to lawyers. Yet, you should not neglect the skill of being able to find similarities between cases. Sometimes we call that harmonizing cases.

The ability to find common ground in situations of potential conflict has uses in the law that go beyond case analysis. Since we have observed that lawyers are argumentative, and since much of the argument in which lawyers engage concerns the comparison of similarities and differences between cases or problems, it merits emphasis that one of the most useful attributes of many talented lawyers lies in their knack of helping adversaries to narrow and reconcile their differences and to achieve agreement.

Here is a way that the ability to analogize cases may be helpful on the intellectual side of law. We begin by borrowing an example from a famous torts case. Assume that a court has decided that it is a battery if a twelve-year-old boy playfully kicks a classmate during school hours, seriously aggravating a previous wound to the classmate's knee that is concealed by his trousers. The court reasons that the kicker's intent to make a contact was sufficient to constitute a battery, even if the young defendant did not intend harm to his classmate. In the model of case analysis we are developing, that decision provides the rule, which for these purposes we might state as being that an intended contact in violation of social norms is a battery.

Now consider a later case, in which a male employee "affectionately" hugs a female co-worker, who has made plain that she dislikes on-the-job hugs. The female employee suffers an immediate and unexpected facial paralysis, which medical testimony indicates was a fortuitous result of the hug.

On the surface, these two cases might sound like they do not have a lot in common—horseplay by kick in an elementary school classroom and an employee hugging a co-worker in the workplace. When we analyze the cases together, however, we can begin to see that they share a common legal thread. Both cases involve a deliberate contact, by someone who subjectively may have thought he was just "fooling around," which causes an objectively unforeseeable but serious physical injury. Thus, one might contend that the cases are analogous, and that the hug, as well as the kick, was a battery. To be sure, there may be room for argument about whether the cases are enough alike that they should come out the same way. Reasoning by analogy, like induction, is a matter of probabilities, not certainty. We are pointing out only that lawyers use reasoning by analogy to see potentially crucial similarities between cases, as well as to synthesize a generally applicable rule.

Distinguishing Cases

Thus far we have focused on ways that lawyers find similarities between and among cases. Inductive reasoning and the particular technique of case synthesis use common threads of cases to develop rules. Deductive reasoning applies generalities developed by synthesis to particular cases that share common elements with the cases from which rules developed. The use of analogy is largely, although not exclusively, a method for revealing similarities in cases. Many times, however, attorneys and judges find it necessary to identify controlling distinctions between cases. A time-honored way for a lawyer to argue that an earlier decision does not control present litigation, and for a court to decide that an earlier decision does not bind it, is to *distinguish* the precedent.

The technique of distinguishing cases presents a kind of reverse image to reasoning by analogy. Instead of using analogy to show how a case at issue is like a previous case, the attorney or judge will stress what he regards as relevant differences between the cases. An example might begin with a precedent that reversed a conviction for distributing pornography, in which the court relied on the free speech clause of the First Amendment. Let us now assume a case that involves a conviction for inflammatory remarks about African-American persons, in a context in which officials feared that the remarks would incite listeners to riot. The defendants in the hate speech case who made the remarks would submit that the pornography precedent required a reversal of their conviction. A court that affirmed their conviction would disagree, saying that pornography does not usually involve the kind of immediate provocation to potentially harmful action typified by a riot, and thus is a more protected kind of speech than racially inflammatory remarks. A court that responded that way would reject arguments based on the idea that pornography has a tendency to generate sexual assaults, perhaps saying that any such harmful effects would not typically occur so immediately or with such far-reaching effects as a riot triggered by race-baiting. This is an example of "distinguishing cases"—showing that the case before the court differs from the precedent in legally relevant ways.

Alternative Arguments

A form of reasoning that lawyers use that often perplexes first-year law students is that of an alternative argument. An example of an alternative argument is one in which a lawyer, defending a client in a contract case, first says to the court, "This contract is invalid because it is unconscionable," giving reasons why the contract is unconscionable. Then, however, she continues, "Second, even if the contract is not unconscionable and is valid, my client did not breach it," and gives reasons why the client did not breach. In alternative argument, the lawyer sets up a logical chain of claims or defenses available to the client or to the opposing party and then analyzes and argues each in turn. The lawyer concedes the first point (the contract is valid and not unconscionable) for the purposes of argument in order to reach the next issue (my client did not breach the contract), but uses the concession only for that purpose. Another example of an alternative argument, with a constitutional basis, is this: A person charged with disturbing the peace argues first that she did not violate the statute, and then argues as an alternative that even if she did, she still cannot be convicted because the statute infringes her right to free speech and thus violates the First Amendment.

Being Relevant

One of the most crucial skills for any lawyer to develop—really, for anyone in ordinary life to develop—is the art of being relevant. Especially for law students whose prior education has consisted largely of giving back memorized facts to the teacher, this will take some learning. Relevance, for these purposes, consists in saying things that properly apply to a particular situation, for example, identifying the particular statutory language that applies to the facts of a problem, or emphasizing facts that are crucial to proving or disproving a particular contention.

The law of evidence provides a gatekeeping function for trials that is based on relevance. Consider, as a fanciful introductory illustration, a trial of a man for murdering his wife. The prosecutor seeks to introduce evidence that the defendant once was engaged to eight women at the same time. This evidence is irrelevant and no court will admit it. Although these facts might put the defendant in a bad light with some jurors, there is no logical linkage between evidence of multiple engagements and a tendency to murder a spouse.

One might contrast an evidentiary question that arose in the much publicized trial of O.J. Simpson for murdering his ex-wife and another victim. The issue was whether the prosecution could introduce evidence that Simpson abused his wife in the years before the murder. The court admitted some of the evidence on the basis that it was relevant to whether the defendant had a tendency to commit violent acts against his wife. Whether you agree or not, you probably will conclude that this evidence presents a much stronger case for the prosecution than the hypothetical evidence of prior engagements.

The Use of Hypotheticals

Most law teachers use hypothetical cases to develop a topic. You may get tired of "hypos." You may say to yourself, "Why doesn't she give us the rule instead of making us jump through hoops?" Or, as one of us heard a student say to the professor in the first-year contracts class she had as a student, "You can answer that; it's just 'yes' or 'no.'"

We offer here a couple of responses to these irritated reactions. First, hypotheticals are the way that many professors operate, so you might as well grin and bear it. But the reason you might as well grin, as well as bear it, is important. Practicing lawyers really do operate, almost as a reflex, by asking questions of themselves and of others, about hypothetical cases—the cases just across the line from the actual one they are dealing with. A principal reason they do that is because they may be called to account by adversaries and judges. Opponents will try to embarrass you with hypotheticals to show up the flaws in your logic: "If the court holds for you in this case, it will have to hold for Party X in this hypothetical case, and wouldn't that be stupid?" Judges themselves may put hypos to you to help sharpen their own thinking about the limits of your claim or defense. Your partners, if they are good partners, will put them to you to prepare you for what judges, or opponents, may ask. If you are on your own, you would do well to create your own hypotheticals. Ultimately, someone else will.

There are two particular values in hypotheticals that relate to points we made earlier in this chapter. First, they help you to reason by analogy. Is this case enough like a precedent case to make them legally comparable, so that the rule of the prior case should apply, and the party whose position is analogous to that of the victor in the first case should win? Second, they force you to a test of relevance: Does the precedent I want to invoke persuasively apply to the case before me now, and in which specific ways?

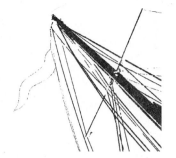

7

Interpreting Language

Law school, and law generally, provide both challenges and opportunities in the use of language. In law school, the difficulty of the challenge will depend in part on your prior experience with the plastic possibilities of words. In practice, your ability to use language creatively will create unlimited opportunities.

The Same Word May Mean Different Things

Words that you have grown up believing have particular, rather fixed meanings—"ordinary" meanings—may turn out in legal contexts to stand for things that are different from what they signified to you before. We will give just a couple of examples that will take on more significance when your teachers put flesh on them in concrete legal contexts.

Consider the word "intent." Most readers without exposure to the law probably think they have a well-defined idea of what "intent" means—something like a fixed purpose to accomplish a goal. As you plow into legal terminology, however, you will learn that intent does not simply mean purpose, or desire. It may also mean something a little less purposeful—for example, in the law of torts, it may mean acting with substantial certainty that a particular result will occur.

A "substantial certainty" definition of intent will control the outcome in particular cases. An example, borrowed from a precedent, is a case in which a small child pulled a chair out from under an elderly woman, who suffered serious injuries in the resulting fall. A jury might decide that the child did not have a specific purpose to cause the plaintiff to fall, but that on the basis of his life experience, he would have been substantially certain that she would fall as a result of his pulling out the chair. Thus, if a court defined "intent" to include "substantial certainty" rather than only "desire" or "purpose," it would open the gate a little wider to claims for personal injury based on "intent."

Another illustration concerns the word "malice." Most people probably have a pretty fixed idea that "malice" means something like "spite," implying a sense of vindictiveness. As you get into the language of the law, however, it will become clear that courts give several meanings to this one word. For example, in the area of defamation law, the Supreme Court has endowed the term with a very specific meaning. Instead of necessarily signifying spite or vicious intentions, the word "malice" may mean "reckless disregard of the truth or falsity" of a remark that injures reputation. The harm caused by a reckless publication of defamatory remarks is not pleasant to contemplate, but it may not necessarily involve the kind of malice that most people associate with that word. Thus, the definition of "malice" to include "reckless disregard" may permit more suits than a definition that requires spite.[1]

The law can complicate one word even more; a court might use the term malice in two different ways in the same defamation case. For one purpose—determining whether an action can be brought for defaming someone in the public eye—the word may mean "reckless disregard." For another purpose—the decision of whether to award punitive damages—it might mean something more like "spite." Thus, one could be found to have published a defamatory statement with "malice" in the sense of "reckless disregard," justifying an award of compensatory damages in favor of a public official, but not with the kind of vindictive "malice" to justify punitive damages. We must add that interestingly enough—really, confusingly—the Supreme Court has defined "reckless disregard" by the term "actual malice," a usage that you might ordinarily think would accentuate the require-

---

[1] As a matter of constitutional law, the Supreme Court's use of the "malice" standard in this context actually limited the opportunities that previously existed for certain people to sue for defamation. Our point, however, is that the Court's use of the term "malice" is generally broader than the ordinary connotations of the word.

ment that a claimant must show spite or vindictiveness. This simply underlines the point that words often have meanings in the law that are not their "ordinary" meanings.

Interpreting Language

A good part of the job of courts and of lawyers is to interpret words and phrases. Rather vague phrases like "equal protection of the laws," or "due process of law," or "cruel and unusual punishment" do not come to us defined for all time and all situations. Is it "cruel and unusual punishment" to impose the death penalty on a murderer? There is a difference of opinion on that question. Is it a deprivation of employees' "due process of law" to limit the hours that they may work? Early in the century, there were serious differences of opinion on that issue. Courts must resolve disputes over the meaning of words by interpreting language of this sort.

In addition to their role in deciphering such abstract phrases, courts also must determine the meaning of words that superficially seem less vague, but still require interpretation. Consider, for example, a "statute of repose" that bars lawsuits beyond a certain period of years with respect to defects in "improvements to real property." If a factory is real property, and a crane by itself is a very large piece of personal property, is a crane that has been installed in a factory an "improvement to real property"? There has been some disagreement on this issue, with the courts focusing on such questions as the permanence with which the crane is attached to the factory premises, how crucial the machine is to the operation of the plant, and whether it was custom-designed for incorporation into that particular plant. Thus, even a fairly straightforward statutory term like "improvement to real property" requires interpretation, and in litigation, it is courts that must supply its meaning.

Stretching Words

Although lawyers always have to interpret words and give them content, you may come to think that they sometimes try to stretch words, and that sometimes courts do stretch them. An example comes from the Constitution's grant to Congress of power to regulate commerce "among the several States." Until the nineteen thirties, most people would have given that phrase a relatively literal meaning, calling up images of vehicles or persons actually moving across state lines. Imagine, then, the surprise of an Ohio farmer who challenged a penalty imposed on him under a federal statute for exceeding the statute's marketing quota for wheat grown on his farm. To what must have been the farmer's dismay, the Supreme Court said that his production beyond his quota had a potential impact on prices of wheat that moved in interstate commerce that was significant enough that Congress' power to regulate that commerce extended to his individual farm. In fact, the Court said that the marketing quota constitutionally could cover even wheat "consumed on the premises," as food for livestock and flour for home baking. The Court reasoned that wheat that the farmer consumed himself "supplies a need...which would otherwise be reflected by purchases in the open market."[2] This famous decision illustrates that one of the reasons that lawyers are wonderful folks—or people who twist the truth, depending on your point of view in a particular case—is that they can give this kind of content to words.

There are limits. Courts would not interpret a statute that specifically allows an administrative agency to regulate the labeling of refrigerators to empower it to regulate the labeling of automobiles. Would a statute that permits an agency to regulate safety in the "workplace" permit it to promulgate regulations for the safety of domestic workers in homes? That might not be out of the question, because a home may be a workplace, although it is not a likely result. But one does not have to answer that question to appreciate the plasticity of language in the law.

A more complex example appears in a much-discussed recent decision in which the Supreme Court said that a statute exceeded the power of Congress to regulate interstate commerce. At issue in this case was the Gun-Free School Zones Act, which made it a federal crime knowingly to possess a firearm in a place that the defendant knew or reasonably believed was a school zone. The defendant in

---

[2] Wickard v. Filburn, 317 U.S. 111 (1942).

this case was convicted under that statute because he brought a .38 handgun to his San Antonio high school. A majority of the Court decided that the legislation was unconstitutional and affirmed an appellate court's reversal of the conviction. The Court said the "the possession of a gun in a local school zone is in no sense an economic activity" that by repetition of that behavior "might . . . substantially affect any sort of interstate commerce."[3] The Court took into account its decision in the case of the wheat farmer, which it said was "perhaps the most far reaching example of Commerce Clause authority over intrastate activity," but distinguished that case because it "involved economic activity in a way that the possession of a gun in a school zone does not."[4]

Using Policies to Define Words and Phrases

When courts confront a dispute about the meaning of legal terms, for example if a term is ambiguous, that is, capable of more than one meaning, they often will interpret the words to harmonize with the policies in which these terms are rooted. A legislative example involves a statute that revokes a person's will made prior to marriage unless "provision was made for the surviving spouse by settlement before or during marriage, or the survivor is provided for in the will." (The effect of such a revocation of a will is that the surviving spouse inherits a share of the estate that is defined by statute.) Mr. and Ms. Green signed a settlement agreement before their marriage that provided that neither spouse would claim any inheritance rights to the other's property. Mr. Green had a premarital will that did not include Ms. Green. He did not change that will after they were married, and thus died with that document being his will.

When Mr. Green died, Ms. Green was destitute, having forfeited her seniority and pension when she left her job at her husband's insistence. She claimed that Mr. Green's premarital will was revoked by the statute because he had made no provision for her, arguing that to make "provision" meant to give property. Thus, she contended, she was entitled to a statutory inheritance as his surviving spouse.

---

[3] United States v. Lopez, 115 S. Ct. 1624, 1634 (1995).
[4] Id. at 1630.

Mr. Green's administrator, acting on behalf of the estate, claimed that Mr. Green had made "provision" because the couple's premarital agreement was a settlement, and that "provision" meant only that the decedent made prior preparations concerning the spouse. The dictionary defines "provision" as having both meanings: "the state of being prepared" (supporting the estate's position), and also "a gift" (supporting Ms. Green).

The court presented with this problem agreed with the estate's argument that the statutory term "provision" meant only "make preparations." It decided that this was the meaning of the term because it determined that the policy behind the statutory language "provision was made" was one of guarding against unintentional disinheritance. Had the court decided that the purpose of the statute was a different one, for example, to ensure support for a surviving spouse, it would, no doubt, have interpreted the statute differently. However a court might interpret the particular term "provision" in a case like that involving Mr. Green's will, the point is that courts make use of the policy behind the law to interpret the words that are the language of the law. We shall elaborate on judicial use of policy in Chapters 8, 9 and 10.

Interpreting Statutes

A lot of the work that first-year law students do involves common law, but that should not obscure the fact that a substantial amount of practicing lawyers' work consists of reading and interpreting statutes. Many students are apprehensive about analyzing statutory topics. Although some of the preceding material in this Chapter deals with statutes, this Part specifically introduces some basic steps of statutory analysis and by doing so, seeks to relieve some of that anxiety.

Read the Statute

Point one would also be point 100, if we had space to make 100 points. It is obvious as it can be. It is also very difficult for law students to believe its literal truth. *Read the statute.* Say it again with emphasis, with an added rule: READ THE STATUTE AND NOTE ITS EXACT LANGUAGE.

It may be useful to introduce a contrasting point. When you are briefing an appellate case, it often may be a good idea to paraphrase what the court said. That way you force yourself to put the court's conclusion into your own words. By contrast, that is not a good idea when you are reading a statute. There may eventually be room for interpretation, but you start with the exact words of the legislature. Never try to paraphrase a statute.

Failure to read a statute, and to take seriously its exact language, is one of the errors that students make most often. The point may not come across until you make a few mistakes of that kind. There will come a time, however, when the idea that you must read statutory language exactly will have worn a groove in your brain.

After you have familiarized yourself with a statute, look for the particular statutory language that your assignment involves and focus on that part of the statute. The case that you read for class, or the problem you have for your writing assignment, will require you to analyze how that specific language applies to particular facts.

Plain Meaning

Lawyers use some fairly standard techniques to interpret statutes. Although the actual interpretation is sometimes difficult, students may easily grasp the basic techniques.

First, not surprisingly, the most obvious step is to look for the plain meaning of the statutory language. The crux of the "plain meaning rule" is that, if the language has a plain meaning, then the court will not analyze any evidence of what the statute means. It must interpret the language using only the statute itself. The plain meaning rule is really a "no extrinsic evidence" rule: the court will not consider evidence extrinsic to—that is, outside of—the statute. For example, if a statute permits a seller of goods to disclaim all responsibility for injury caused by its goods only if the disclaimer is written in red ink in one-inch type, the seller cannot introduce evidence that the legislature really meant only that the disclaimer must be conspicuous.

Another example of "plain meaning" would treat the Constitution of the United States as a statute. Consider Article II, section 1 of the Constitution, which says, speaking of the President, "neither shall any Person be eligible to that office who shall not have attained to the Age of thirty five Years."

Suppose that an exceptionally serious and able young politician who is 33 years old comes to you and says he wants to run for President. He argues that the phrase "thirty five Years" was just a way in which the makers of the Constitution expressed their opinion that the President should be a mature person with ripe experience in public life. He asks why he can't argue that the "thirty five" requirement is a guideline and not a hard and fast rule. Your answer would have to be that he must wait one more election to try for the Oval Office. "Thirty five" has a plain meaning: thirty five.

Although we have provided these illustrations, we should emphasize that words rarely have just one meaning, and that some words that are "plain" to people in one area of life may not be plain to people in another. As is apparent from our example in section IV about the wills statute, even the seemingly simple phrase "make provision" has two recognized meanings—to prepare for or to make a gift. Many words take their meanings from context. The word "estate" in a deed or contract might refer to a particular piece of property. The same word in a will might mean all that a person owned at death.

Legislative History

If statutory language does not have one plain meaning, and it often does not, then the court will analyze extrinsic evidence, that is, evidence of the legislative intent, to determine what the legislature meant by that language. Indeed, recent interpretations permit courts to consider such extrinsic evidence even if the statute may have a plain meaning, in order to determine if the legislature simply could not have intended the plain meaning. The type of evidence most often used to determine legislative intent is the legislative history, that is, the documented trail of information left as the statute made its way through the legislative process. This trail includes the introduction of the statute as a bill, its consideration by a committee, the committee vote, the vote on the floor of the legislature, and then signature by the executive. Each of these stages of the process produces some documentation, for example, legislative committee reports. Congressional committees often publish extensive reports concerning bills that become federal legislation. All of this material may yield some clues to the intended meaning of the statute's language. Sometimes the clues are explicit explanations; often, however, they are not, and the lawyer must create a story, based on a view of the purpose of the statute that is favorable to her client, about how the language should be interpreted.

Other types of evidence about the meaning of legislation may come from other parts of the same statute or from other, similar statutes. If the legislature used the exact language at issue in other sections of the disputed statute, or the same language in other statutes on similar subjects, then a lawyer would interpret that language to be consistent in its meaning throughout the statute. If, however, the legislature used similar, but different, language elsewhere in the statute, then perhaps it intended to impart different meanings to those terms.

Another indirect kind of evidence would be failed amendments, which give an idea of language the legislature did not intend to adopt. An illustration follows from our example above about disclaimers on the sale of goods. Assume that when the legislature specifically said that disclaimers should be written in red ink in one-inch type, it rejected a proposed amendment that said that disclaimers would be effective only if they were "conspicuous." The rejected amendment would add support to the argument that the requirement of red ink and one-inch type is the exclusive means of creating an effective disclaimer.

Many lawyers who represent clients interested in proposed legislation will spend part of their time creating legislative histories. They will, for example, formulate questions for one senator to ask another senator during debate on the Senate floor about the meaning of a particular phrase in a bill, and will also fashion appropriate responses. These statements are published in the Congressional Record and become part of the legislative history. Questions of interpretation arise when there are conflicting statements of that sort in the legislative history of a bill.

As is evident throughout this chapter, the language of legislation is often ambiguous or elastic. That may sometimes be a result of careless or hurried drafting. Often, however, it may reflect the fact that legislation, by its nature, represents a compromise between warring forces. Statutory language may be ambiguous because it was necessary for proponents of legislation to make some ideas fuzzy in order to entice enough supporters to pass a bill. The basic point is that legislative history is a tool that courts use for interpretive help when the meaning of statutes becomes the subject of litigation. Proponents of legislation have that in mind when they draft the question-and-answer dramas by which members of Congress "explain" the "meaning" of a bill.

Canons of Statutory Construction

You would use the analysis we have outlined above to interpret the purpose of a legislature as it reflects specifically on the meaning of a particular statute. Another type of analysis is that of statutory construction. The goal of this approach is to construct what is usually meant by a particular kind of language, or by a particular type of statute, when the person doing the interpretation does not know what was actually intended. This process uses what are known as canons of construction.

Below we give four examples of these canons, presented in rough pairings of ideas. The first canon is the idea that the expression of one thing excludes other things not mentioned. The second is the concept that when a general word follows a list of specific things, persons interpreting the language may look to the specific list to give meaning to the general word. The third and fourth canons are, respectively, that courts should narrowly construe statutes "in derogation of the common law," and that courts should broadly construe "remedial statutes."

Expressio Unius

Although we have strived to keep this book completely in English, we will make a small bow to legal Latin and introduce the canon, "Expressio unius est exclusio alterius." That means, roughly, that to express one thing—at least in a statute—is to exclude other things that have not been mentioned.

Assume that a statute makes it a misdemeanor to let "swine, cattle, or sheep run at large." The sheriff arrests Mr. X because he finds Mr. X's goat on the highway, but the prosecutor tells the sheriff to let Mr. X go because the law does not support the arrest. The sheriff might argue, "I know the law says swine, cattle, or sheep, but goats are close enough." The prosecutor will emphasize to the sheriff that this statute makes it a crime—even though a minor crime—to let certain livestock run loose. Because of the stigma associated with crime, the prosecutor will explain that one must assume that in making a very specific list, the legislature meant only to punish the exact behaviors on that list, and to exclude all others. It is true that the legislature in fact may not have intended its list to be exclusive. However, the prosecutor might also explain her decision not to prosecute by referring to another canon, one that says that criminal statutes should be strictly construed. The reason supporting this canon is that a person should not be punished for a crime unless he has clear warning in the statute that the conduct is criminal.

Ejusdem Generis

Another canon of statutory construction—one more Latin phrase—might have applied if the statute had made it a crime to allow "swine, cattle, or sheep, or other such animals to run at large." In that case, a court could apply the statute to goats by using the canon known as *ejusdem generis*, which means of the same genus or class, and applies to catch-all words after an enumerated list. Animals could be of the same kind as the three listed creatures if they are four-legged and are common farm animals, such as a goat.

However, given that the three listed animals are also commonly used for human consumption, and if goat meat is not usually eaten by people in that jurisdiction, then a court might conclude that the statute does not include goats. That would be because under an interpretation that focused on the common characteristic of the listed animals as livestock used for food, goats would not be of the same class as the other three animals. The statute also might not apply to a dog or cat because they are domesticated animals. If you want to pose to yourself a more difficult question, ask how a court should respond to the case of a pig that a farm family has adopted as a house pet.

Narrow Construction of Statutes in Derogation of the Common Law

Another principle of statutory construction fits rather closely here. This is the maxim that when a statute goes beyond the common law, courts should interpret it narrowly.

An example from civil litigation concerns tort damages. Let us say that the common law in a particular state allows theoretically unlimited damages for intangible harms connected with physical injury. The legislature, seeking to cut back on tort remedies, enacts a statute that limits injury victims to $500,000 for "pain and suffering." A jury makes an award to an injured plaintiff that includes an item of one million dollars, labeled as representing "loss of capacity to enjoy life." The defendant seeks to reduce this award by $500,000, invoking the statutory cap on "pain and suffering" damages.

The defendant would argue that when the legislature used the phrase "pain and suffering," it had in mind a broad cluster of intangible harms that cannot easily be quantified in dollars. A court, however, might well refuse to apply the "pain and suffering" cap to "loss of capacity to enjoy life." Since the statute cuts back on common law remedies—to use the more sonorous phrase, the statute is "in derogation of the common law"—the court probably (although not undoubtedly) would construe the legislation against the party who is relying on it, that is, the defendant. The court might explain that if the legislature had intended to limit "loss of capacity" damages, it knew how to say so, but didn't.

One should note, incidentally, that the great maxims of statutory construction often tend to spill over into one another. For a court to construe this statute narrowly could be said, in effect, to apply the canon "expressio unius": to express "pain and suffering" is to exclude all other forms of injury. Some might even argue that this interpretation applies the "plain meaning" rule.

Broad Construction of Remedial Statutes

A somewhat contrasting idea is that courts should broadly construe "remedial" statutes. Assume that in a particular jurisdiction, the courts have never allowed damage claims for water pollution, effectively responding to the dependence of the state's economy on its chemical industry. They also have never allowed nuisance claims for offensive animal odors, indirectly recognizing that the second most important industry in the state is livestock farming.

With the passage of time, however, the state becomes progressively urban and suburban, and homeowners whose houses sit near rivers begin complaining to their legislators about chemicals in the streams. After hearings that amass information on the public perils and inconveniences of toxic and ill-smelling chemicals, the legislature passes a statute that permits private damage actions for "air and water pollution."

There is legislative history that suggests that the legislature hardly thought about "air pollution," because it was concentrating on the contamination of water by chemicals; a drafter of the statute included "air" in the bill because it just seemed more comprehensive. However, along comes a suburban homeowner who complains that the odors of a nearby pig sty make life very unpleasant for his family. He sues the owner of the sty for violating the pollution statute. The sty owner will argue that in passing the statute, the legislature really was not targeting air pollution. Moreover, he will point out that the primary evil that the legislative hearings addressed was that of chemical pollution. Thus, he will contend, at most "air . . . pollution" means pollution by environmental chemicals, not the smell of pigs. Yet, though residents of the state previously could not have brought claims for animal odors, the court might well (although not necessarily) construe the words "air . . . pollution" to include the aroma from the pig sty. If it does, it probably will rely on the idea that a statute that is avowedly remedial should be construed broadly.

If it has occurred to you that sometimes maxims of statutory construction clash with one another, congratulate yourself. Naturally, the sty owner would argue that because the state's courts did not allow suits on animal odors before the passage of the statute, the court should construe the statute narrowly. Thus, arguably we now have two maxims in conflict—a narrow construction rule for statutes that change the common law and a maxim of broad construction for remedial statutes.

You should get used to this kind of conflict and uncertainty. Moreover, you should view it as good news. It is exactly this sort of ambiguity—and the room for creative argument that it offers—that provides employment for lawyers.

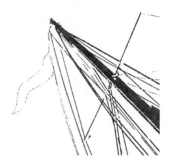

8

Balancing Competing Interests and Factors

A great deal of law—and specifically for our present purposes, of the work of courts—consists of weighing and balancing. For example, courts weigh the parties' competing legal interests, and relevant facts in particular situations, to determine which party has proved his case.

Law as Influencing Behavior

Many decisions that the law makes to resolve disputes, and to deal with the underlying conflicts of social and economic policy, proceed on the assumption that law influences behavior. This premise underlies many rules of law, contained both in statutes and judge-made rules. Ordinarily, we hardly think about many of the ways that law affects conduct, so much are they a part of our lives.

Consider a few obvious examples:

- Many rules of contract law force us into formalities that we might not otherwise observe: Put it in writing. Sign both copies. Don't bury important ideas in the fine print.

- Tort rules guide conduct by informing us what level of risk
  is socially unacceptable: Do not drive over the speed limit,
  or you will have to pay those you injure. Do not let produce
  accumulate on your supermarket floor, or you may have to
  compensate those who slip and get hurt. Those two examples, directly embodying disincentives for undesired conduct, illustrate negative advice aimed at "deterrence." Tort
  law also effectively communicates advice about desirable
  conduct like, "Doctor, listen to your patients." Ordinarily,
  we might not think of that as a deterrence-oriented suggestion, since it tells someone what to do, rather than what not
  to do. However, as is the case with classic negative deterrence, the key is behavior control, since the clear implication
  is that one ignores the advice at the risk of malpractice suits.

- The criminal law goes beyond the law of torts: Don't drive
  over the speed limit, or you may go to jail. Absolutely,
  don't drive while drunk, or you may go to jail for a long
  time. Thou shalt not kill, and if you do, you may be executed. Even, thou shalt not cheat. These illustrations represent, once more, negatively framed deterrence. Again, too,
  the law in effect offers some positive advice, for example,
  keep good records of your company's sales. Here an im-
  plied threat for noncompliance is the risk of a prosecution
  for tax fraud. Framed in terms of what to do, rather than
  what not to do, such counsel embodies an incentive to avoid
  unpleasant treatment by officials.

- The rules of property law advise us about all manner of behavior: Have your land surveyed so there are no disagreements about where the fence belongs. If you own a parcel
  of land but do not actively use it, visit it now and then to signal your ownership. Do not keep pigs in suburbia.

- The rules of procedure also influence conduct: Do not file a
  claim unless you have found some law to support your case,

or the court may impose sanctions on you. File your motions on time. Do not continue a litigation if you come up short on evidence. Even, think about settling this case.

Balancing of Interests

If we view law as a set of rules for governing human behavior, we need not reach beyond everyday experience to understand that a principal reason we need those rules is to minimize conflict. Even casual observation of daily life reveals frequent interactions between and among people that will cause disputes or exhibit potential for interpersonal controversy. The seller of corporate stock that neglects to tell a buyer that the corporation is being sued for everything it owns; the motorist whose fast driving causes a fatal injury; the "night-person" homeowner in a community of small lots who blasts his sound equipment at 3 a.m.—all these situations present cases likely to require "dispute resolution."

In resolving disputes and fashioning rules, American courts more or less consciously attempt to balance the competing interests of parties.

Some of the cases we mentioned provide illustrations of this process of weighing and balancing:

- The problem of whether a seller of stock must tell a purchaser about events that create significant risks to the corporate treasury underlines the difficulty that the law often faces in deciding how much information a seller must give to a prospective buyer. A strong element of our moral traditions condemns cheating and "sharp practice." But another, somewhat competing element, urges that buyers must be self-reliant. An economic perspective suggests that the answer to the question of how much information one party to a sales transaction must give to another depends on how much it would cost each to obtain the information.

Yet several factors may complicate the analysis of comparative information costs. For example, in ordinary consumer transactions a low-income purchaser may find it difficult, or impossible, to acquire information. An uneducated consumer, or one who does not understand English, may not be able to absorb or process relevant information. Courts must balance many factors like these when they decide whether, for example, a sales transaction was "unconscionable."

- The law must weigh facts and policies when dealing with conduct that physically injures a person. Consider, for example, the case of a speeding motorist who runs into a pedestrian and kills her. Since the driver was speeding, the criminal law may punish him in some way, and the pedestrian's family may sue the motorist for the financial consequences of her death. But should the criminal punishment be a fine? If so, how much? Should it also involve jail time? Should the money that the motorist must pay the victim's family be measured on a "compensatory" scale alone, or should it include "punitive" damages, which themselves serve a kind of "punishment" purpose?   What precisely were the facts? Just how fast was the motorist driving? In how densely populated an area? Was he drunk or under the influence of a controlled substance? Was he driving in a way that distinguished his behavior from a manner in which almost every motorist drives at some time in any given month? Was he driving at the speed at which most motorists drive on that stretch of highway most of the time, which happens to exceed the posted speed limit by ten miles per hour? What will be the likely effect on that particular driver's future conduct of a specific form of criminal punishment or a particular amount of civil damages? What will be its effect on drivers in general?

In cases of this sort, courts must weigh assumptions about the behavioral effects of different kinds of remedies, the social consensus (if one is discernable) about the level of culpability of particular types of conduct, and a general sense of how people in society would react to a particular type of penalty or award. When a trial judge says, "five years in jail," or an appellate court affirms a judgment for $150,000 compensatory damages and $500,000 punitive damages, they are balancing all these considerations.

- The need to balance competing property interests is evident in the case of the homeowner who uses a very loud stereo well into the wee hours of the morning. If you are his neighbor, you would see only one right. That is, a right rooted in your interest in peace and quiet after a reasonable hour—what *you* think of as a reasonable hour. If you are the stereo owner, you would see yourself as exercising an important right—the right to use your property as you wish. Maybe you would even believe, and certainly your lawyer would argue, that you are somehow exercising your right to free expression. When courts decide nuisance cases, or when city councils write noise regulation ordinances, they balance these rights. A city council probably will set rough guidelines about when someone can generate loud noises. It may impose outright prohibitions on some forms of noise. For other kinds of noise, it may announce quantitative standards, for example, rules expressed in terms of decibel levels. Each of these decisions represents a social weighing of interests in conflict.

- A further example, from the area of constitutional law, concerns the law of defamation and its relation to the First Amendment's prohibition of restrictions on speech. Some analysts of free speech issues argue for an "absolutist" position, saying essentially that there is never a persuasive reason for government to regulate speech, even defamatory speech. Others insist, by contrast, that it is exactly the role of courts to weigh competing interests and the policies that support them. These commentators would say, for example, that despite the attraction of the idea that the cure for vicious speech is always more speech, sometimes speech becomes so offensive or harmful that its destructive effects outweigh the social interest served by freedom of communication.

The Concept of Factor Analysis

An approach that parallels the balancing of interests in the setting of legal standards is the technique of factor analysis. Where the balancing of interests may evoke the metaphor of a scale and two sets of weights, the technique of factor analysis might trigger the image of a smorgasbord menu. It enables the court to draw upon a catalog of several factors, sometimes presented as a list, from which it selects what it considers the most relevant factor or factors as the basis for its decision. The sources of this catalog may be prior judicial decisions or statutes.

It is useful to have in mind the way in which a cause of action that involves factor analysis differs from one defined by elements. An elements claim, such as a cause of action for an intentional tort like battery, requires the plaintiff to prove each element of the definition of that claim, for example, intent, contact, and lack of consent. By contrast, in the case of a cause of action that involves factors, the plaintiff will offer facts that relate to those factors, but her success will not necessarily depend on presenting proof under each factor. Rather, the successful plaintiff will convince the court that she has shown that the circumstances of the case are favorable with respect to the most important factor or factors in the list, or that, on balance, her proof satisfies enough factors to outweigh the opposing claim.

An illustration appears in the area of suits for pollution by chemicals in the environment. A question that sometimes arises in these cases is whether the court should impose strict liability on a polluter, that is, liability without fault, rather than requiring the plaintiff to prove that the defendant was negligent. Some courts require plaintiffs who wish to use a strict liability theory to show that the defendant's conduct was "abnormally dangerous," a phrase borrowed from section 519 of the Restatement (Second) of Torts.

This Restatement standard requires courts to consider six factors, enumerated in section 520:

(a) existence of a high degree of risk of some harm to the person, land or chattels of others;
(b) likelihood that the harm that results from [the defendant's activity] will be great;
(c) inability to eliminate the risk by the exercise of reasonable care;
(d) extent to which the activity is not a matter of common usage;
(e) inappropriateness of the activity to the place where it is carried on; and
(f) extent to which its value to the community is outweighed by its dangerous attributes." [1]

This list is an example of how detailed a factor analysis can be. A court that adopts the section 520 approach must consider each factor and engage in a balancing process. For example, it might find that the first five factors all weigh in the plaintiff's favor. It would then have to weigh such considerations as the great danger of an activity and its lack of "fit" in a community against the value of the activity to the community.

Legislatures also write statutes that contain lists of factors for the courts to consider. One typical example is a statute directing courts to divide a couple's marital property between them at divorce, taking into account several relevant factors, including

(1) the contribution of each spouse to the acquisition of the property
(2) the value of other property set apart for each spouse
(3) the duration of the marriage
(4) the economic circumstances of each spouse
(5) the age of each spouse
(6) if there are children of the marriage, the custodial spouse's need for the family home. [2]

---

[1] Restatement (Second) of Torts §520 (1977).
[2] Taken from the original Uniform Marriage and Divorce Act §307.

A court deciding how to apportion the property of a divorcing couple with children, possessing modest means, might decide that a spouse with a job outside the home had the stronger case on element (1), despite the other spouse's contributions in homemaking. It might decide that element (2) counted for nothing because neither spouse had individual property set aside. However, the court might conclude that there was a significant disadvantage to a spouse who had not pursued a career during a long marriage, and who thus argued that it would be difficult to find work. This would cut in favor of that spouse on elements (3), (4) and (5). Moreover, the court might decide that a custodial spouse deserved the bigger split of property because that spouse needed a place to raise the couple's children (element 6).

Some people think that lists of factors are cop-outs—that they provide judges an excuse to do almost anything they please. It might be argued, for example, that a judge deciding a case based on the Restatement's strict liability factors could focus on item (e), say that the defendant's activity was inappropriate to the area in which it was carried on, and declare it unreasonably dangerous without much in the way of explanation—or balancing. Or a family law judge dealing with a division of marital property may think that the economic circumstances of each spouse should dominate all other factors. A major concern of critics is that to allow judges that much discretion leads to a high risk of unpredictable decisions.[3]

Factor analysis does present those risks. However, the discretionary aspect of factor analysis—the way it permits judges to determine the weight of each factor or to choose the most relevant factor from a list—also presents advantages. Indeed, a primary justification for the use of factor analysis is that it forces conscientious judges to focus on the most relevant facts, often including the individual circumstances of the parties, as well as policies and precedents, to determine what truly are the things that count for decision.

Tied in with this justification is the notion that the job of judges is to exercise *judgment*. The law often does not emerge as a neat grid of mechanical rules. The very idea of law, as we have emphasized, arises from dispute and controversy in individual cases. Of course, the law tries to impose order on messes, and appellate review provides

---

[3] See, e.g., George Christie, An Essay on Discretion, 1986 Duke L.J. 747.

some of that order when appellate courts impose guidelines on lower courts' exercise of discretion. But often the result is not an entirely tidy package. Factor analysis can provide a flexible means of sorting out several elements of an intellectually complex situation. The judge who seriously reviews a catalog of decisional factors will be the more honest, and the more persuasive, the more she reveals how she sorted out and ranked those factors.

It is fair to ask how factor analysis relates to the process of judicial weighing and balancing. Properly done, factor analysis results in a form of balancing. Candidly done, it can help judges who write opinions to persuade their readers that they have done justice.

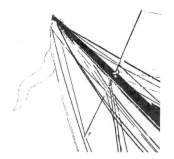

9

Policy Foundations

Non-lawyers probably tend to think of law as a "technical" set of rules. They are not wrong, up to a point. There is a side to law that is relatively mechanical. Here is a mechanical "rule": it is an offense to drive more than 40 miles per hour. Mr. D drives 55. He has broken the rule, and committed an offense. That is syllogistic. The rule is the major premise, Mr. D's conduct supplies the minor premise, and the conclusion is that he has violated the law.

But in more cases than most people might ordinarily think, the law is anything but mechanical. There are exceptions even to the apparently ironclad rule mentioned above. One may drive above the posted speed when operating an emergency vehicle or taking a woman in labor to the hospital. More importantly, one cannot begin to understand or interpret a rule unless one understands the policy basis for the rule. The question is not so much "what?" but "why?"

There are squadrons of policies that underlie various "rules" of law. This chapter does not attempt to present an exhaustive catalog. We do try to identify some of the most important policies, or rationales, for decisionmaking. Although we may not have presented the very one that your professor in torts or contracts or civil procedure will invoke in tomorrow's class, we have put together a number of often mentioned ideas. We suspect that for most students, these concepts will inform, or even dominate, discussion in many of your classes.

Some Basic Jurisprudential Concepts

This section summarizes some basic ideas in the philosophy of law that courts apply to a wide range of specific legal topics.

The Descriptive and the Normative

An introductory point concerns the distinction between "descriptive" or "positive" analysis and "normative" concerns. Many analysts of law concern themselves principally with describing things the way they are. In theory, this is a "scientific" enterprise. In some academic contexts, scholars will refer to this endeavor as "positive" analysis.[1] For the purposes of this summary, the relevant point is that description should not have ideological overtones.

The "normative," by contrast, deals with the "ought." Those who examine the law normatively will make a bow to the "facts" that descriptive analysis turns up (although, of course, on important questions there is likely to be disagreement about what the "facts" are). However, the normative question is, how *should* one decide on a particular matter? Perhaps, for example, an analysis of factory work indicates that production is more efficient in states where employers do not have to pay compensation to workers for industrial injuries than in states that require employers to pay for such injuries. If you accepted the definition of efficiency that was offered in this connection, that might be a "fact." But that "positive analysis" would not necessarily settle the question of whether factory owners *ought* to pay compensation to their injured workers. Such issues present normative questions, and they may not be easy. Indeed, "ought" issues often are difficult ones.

Those opposing compensation may say that as a matter of philosophy, people should take their chances with risks that they freely choose to confront. Those who support compensation might say that compassion for injured workers should outweigh, in this case, a philosophical commitment to freedom of choice. They might argue that from an ethical point of view, the burden of such injuries should be assessed to the enterprise as a cost of doing business. Moreover—just to bring "positive analysis" back into the

---

[1] The term "positive" has several refinements of meaning. A related meaning that you may encounter is one that emphasizes the development of models of reality that produce accurate predictions of real world behavior.

discussion—advocates of compensation might confront a "descriptive" facet of the anti-compensation argument directly and say that it is not a "fact" that workplace risks are "freely" chosen. They might use statistical surveys based on worker interviews to show that "duress" compels employees to accept certain risks concerning which they are not free to choose.

Is the Law Neutral?

An important and continuing argument about the system of justice concerns the question of neutrality of decisionmaking. There is a strong tradition of belief that this should be a principal goal of judges. In the purest version of this view, judges should—and can—put aside their personal biases and make decisions that are free of their own political and ideological conceptions. That is an ideal, but many believe that to strive for it will promote respect for courts and for the law generally.

Counterposed against this view is one that urges frank recognition that judges carry around a lot of baggage of personal experience and philosophy and inevitably will apply their preconceived premises to their decisions. Some people will go further and suggest that judges *ought* to apply their biases, perhaps even arguing that it is quite appropriate for "interest groups" to lobby for the appointment of judges that represent their political points of view.

Schools of Thought and Ideology

Law students should be apprised of an important feature of present academic law that reflects ideological struggles in the world generally, and that relates to the issue of neutrality of decisionmaking. This is the rise of schools of thought about the law that feature avowedly ideological approaches, sometimes focusing on the impact of the law on particular groups. We will briefly discuss some of these approaches, including such schools of thought as feminism, critical legal studies, and critical race theory, in Chapter 10.

Many who take these positions will stress that law and decisionmakers are not, and cannot be, neutral. Indeed, with reference to the criticism that their own positions are ideological, they will respond that the traditional ways of analyzing the law are themselves ideological. They will argue that an especially pernicious quality of traditionalist approaches lies in the way they mesh their ideological content with professions of neutrality.

Reason and Arbitrariness

One idea that recurs throughout the law is that rules require reasons. When we demand the "rationale" for a rule, we are basically asking its proponents to give us reasons for it. Those reasons may be dry and abstract, or they may be full of juice and richly related to life. In either event, when we ask for reasons, we are saying: Persuade us. Convince us. Tell us why we should have this rule.

If you reflect on this idea, you will come to see that it is central to our legal system. To take an exaggerated example, let us say that a police officer discovers Mr. A dead on the sidewalk, and finds Mr. B casually leaning against a utility pole in the next block. Without any other facts, the officer arrests Mr. B for the murder of Mr. A. Could a court allow a conviction of Mr. B for the murder? Why not? Because it would be arbitrary—the very opposite of a reasoned decision. An important hint of how this fits into the law as it actually is applied lies in the fact that such a conviction would violate due process. One of the most fundamental meanings of due process is that the decisionmaker must have a reason for her decision.

Clarity

Another important jurisprudential principle is that the law should be clear. This idea links up with the strong opposition the law manifests to arbitrariness. If the rules are muddled, or vague, they do not give a signal to people about how they should behave. Particularly in the case of rules that impose sanctions for their violation, this is unjust. It is especially important that the criminal law be clear because people should have notice of the kind of behavior that will brand them as criminals.

Notice

The requirement that people should have notice of the law is an independent principle that applies beyond the criminal law. An often used example is the case of the Roman emperor who inscribed the laws so high up on a column that no one could read them. If rules are hidden away, or if they are not clear, then people cannot know them and conform their behavior to them. This is unfair, in addition to often being inefficient. How can you obey a rule when you do not know it exists? Although governments do not have to give direct actual notice of each law to all members of the community, they must publish their laws at all levels: constitutions, statutes, ordinances, and administrative regulations. For example, the federal government publishes the *Federal Register*, a daily collection of proposed and newly adopted administrative rules and regulations. Among other things, the *Federal Register* also publishes presidential documents and notices of public meetings.

Predictability and Stability

An associated goal of the law is that of predictability. The idea that the law should be predictable fits in especially well with the requirements of a business-oriented society. Business persons have to know what the rules are so that they can order their productive lives. Much of the law of contracts revolves around this idea. A lot of current controversy about the effects of tort law turns on assertions that expanded liabilities for personal injury leave businesses uncertain about when they will have to pay compensation for injury and how much they will have to pay.

Yet it is not just business persons who desire predictability in the law. People generally have a stake in rules that are relatively stable and that will be enforced in much the same way from day to day. For example, they count on property rules to uniformly assure them clear title to the homes they purchase and for reliable guidelines about how to make an effective gift. We all make plans—short-range and long-range—based on the ideas that we can know today what the law will be tomorrow and that those who resolve our disputes will behave consistently.

Treating Like Cases Alike

In our discussion of stare decisis, we introduced the idea that like cases should be treated alike. This principle has an obvious linkage to the desire for predictability as well as to respect for precedent. People would like to think that if they behave in a particular way that has been approved or allowed by a prior rule, they can count on having that conduct judged in the way it has previously been judged. One reason for this way of thinking is quite practical. The knowledge that your conduct will be treated as similar conduct has previously been treated helps you to plan your life.

Beyond that, there is a philosophical basis for the principle. It lies in a sense that inconsistency of results on similar facts is simply unjust. You only have to consult your intuition to validate this belief. Ask yourself how you would react to the application of opposing rules to identical events that occurred one month apart. It is a safe bet that you would say, "That is unfair." The principle therefore has an ethical foundation as well as roots in pragmatic needs to develop strategies for business and personal life.

Flexibility in the Law

An important counterweight to such goals as clarity and predictability lies in the idea that the law should be flexible. Haven't you thought, on occasion, that someone in a position of authority was "rigid" or "unbending"? Sometimes following a rule out to its "logical" conclusion does not yield what people would call "justice." It is for that reason that practically everyone values "flexibility" in decisionmakers, at least some of the time, and that the law creates exceptions to rules. It is also for that reason that some legislation requires that courts exercise discretion rather than apply a mechanical rule, although discretionary lawmaking is less predictable than the application of fixed rules. We want the law to be able to bend enough to take particular circumstances into account.

Responsiveness to Social Change

A particular challenge to the effort to keep the law stable and predictable arises from the need to make law responsive to changing social conditions. Rules conceived for simple social and economic situations may fail badly in more complex environments, both with respect to the solution of disputes and the effort to prescribe standards for conduct. We give just a few examples.

- Rules of contract governing acceptance of an offer, designed for an age when the fastest transmission of written information was by the mail, will not always effectively govern a time of fax machines.
- Rules of personal injury law that served a time when most goods were sold face to face must change when confronted with systems of mass production and sales that extend over long chains of distribution.
- Rules of procedure that responded to a time when it was considered "part of the game" to spring surprise evidence on opponents have given way to elaborate systems of discovery of evidence in the possession of the other party.
- Rules of property designed for a society that thought it proper that the eldest son of a family should inherit all its land have been replaced by inheritance rules that distribute property equally among children of both sexes.

These are only illustrations of situations in which courts, and sometimes legislatures, have found that the need to respond to changes in society outweighs the need for predictability and certainty.

The General vs. the Specific

This leads us to an age-old question that runs through the law. Should rules be general or specific? We will begin with a general answer—some of both.

How much care should a supermarket owner take against the risk that a customer will slip on something in the store aisles—a spilled beverage or a stray grape? The answer that the law usually gives is a general one, which some people may say is vague: the standard of conduct for supermarket owners is that of "reasonable care."

We could have a much more specific rule that says that a market is liable if, and only if, it did not have someone clean each aisle where things might spill at least every twelve and one half minutes.

Which rule do you like better? We will guess it is the more general one, because there are so many things one would want to take into account in deciding whether it is appropriate to make a market pay for a slip-and-fall injury: the number of spills, the number of injuries believed to be caused by spills, the average age of the clientele, the policies followed by other markets, the size of the market, the number of employees.

There will, however, be some circumstances in which we would prefer a more precise, even quantitative rule. Perhaps, in certain workplace settings, we would want to say that a barrier that guards against the risk of falls must be 54 inches high. That is not because 54 inches is a magic number. It is because that height represents an estimate about the probability of falls by employees over any lower barrier, perhaps allowing some margin for error, and a practical judgment that that probability would be unacceptable. An important justification for such a rule is that it tells the factory owner just what she has to do. The owner may not much care whether the number is 54, or 50, or 58. She principally wants to be given a specific standard.

Or maybe she does care, because each extra inch of height on the barrier is costly. But it may be worth it to her to have a specific rule rather than one that just says, "use reasonable care," because that general a rule may effectively force her to set up a barrier that is 60 or even 62 inches high, "just to be safe."

Another consideration, which may cut in the other direction, is efficiency in the lawmaking process itself. It may be costly to go out and do surveys about how the average height of workers and the height of barriers relate to accident rates. We might conclude that a general standard like "barriers of reasonable height" would be much cheaper to devise, and not much more costly to enforce, than a rule that specifies barrier heights in inches.

There is no easy "rule" that tells you when to be relatively specific and when to be relatively general. Just be aware that your professors will tease you from time to time with this problem. Understand, moreover, that this is serious teasing, because it reflects the exact kinds of choices that courts and legislatures must make in the everyday world of judging and lawmaking.

The contrasts evident above between the values of predictability and of flexibility, and the tension between the general and the specific, will teach a lesson that is difficult for many law students, but familiar to all lawyers. This is that one must be able to analyze problems through a variety of lenses and be prepared to bring to bear a variety of rationales in the effort to solve problems. The ability to do that is a distinguishing feature of the well-trained law student and the creative lawyer.

Different Kinds of Rationality

Lawyers are fond of demanding rationality in rules. But the content of "rationality" may vary depending on the institutional context. Judges—in particular, appellate judges—are likely to hold other judges—in particular, trial judges—to rather high standards of rationality. They will insist that trial judges adhere to a relatively well-defined legal logic, for example, in ruling on motions and in fashioning jury instructions.

Appellate courts will be somewhat more lenient in setting rationality tests for juries. For example, in affirming some large damages awards for intangible elements of injury like pain and suffering, they may say something like this: "We would not have awarded as much money as this jury did, but we cannot say that the size of the award is 'shocking to the conscience'"—that is, that it is irrational.

Courts also will be relatively lenient when they review certain types of legislation, for example, legislation regulating economic behavior, which they are often called upon to do by litigants who claim that a statute violates a constitutional provision such as the due process clause or the equal protection clause. Reviewing legislation challenged on equal protection grounds, for example, judges might conclude that the statute is personally distasteful to them. However,

courts often will say something like this in refusing to hold unconstitutional statutes dealing with such matters as economic regulation:
"We refuse to sit as a superlegislature to weigh the wisdom of
legislation."[2] Exercising even more self-restraint, the Supreme Court
has declared, "We cannot say that the regulation has no rational
relation to that objective and therefore is beyond constitutional
bounds."[3]

Our general point is that "rationality" has many faces, depending
on the subject matter of disputes and whether courts are reviewing
the product of other judges, of juries, or of legislatures.

Approaches to Justice: Different Lenses

The next three sections briefly summarize three principal approaches to justice. You might liken them to different lenses on a
camera. Each emphasizes certain features of the subject, while
tending to exclude others or put them in the background. (1) "Corrective justice," at least in its pure form, centers on the litigants in a
dispute. (2) "Instrumentalism" emphasizes the need for courts to go
beyond the individual merits of the litigants' claims to consider the
policy consequences of decisions in particular cases, and thus contrasts with the pure concept of corrective justice. (3) "Distributive
justice" represents a much broader idea of entitlement than does
corrective justice, one that applies not only between individuals, but
among classes of persons.

Corrective Justice

The concept of corrective justice enters many discussions of the
law. Volumes have been written on this idea. This brief reference to
the concept aims principally to make you aware of the way that
corrective justice fixes on the relationship between particular parties.
One way to phrase the basic idea of corrective justice is to say that it
centers on redress for wrongs; corrective justice seeks to make things
right between the parties. A central feature of the concept is its
focused response to individualized controversies. Corrective justice
provides a way to sort out rights and wrongs in particular disputes.

---

[2] Ferguson v. Skrupa, 372 U.S. 726 (1963) (refusing to invalidate a statute that regulated "the business
of debt adjusting").
[3] Williamson v. Lee Optical Co., 348 U.S. 483 (1955) (refusing to hold unconstitutional a state statute
that made it unlawful for persons who were not licensed optometrists or ophthalmologists to fit lenses
to a face).

In its most rigorous form, it excludes considerations of "policy" that go beyond the individual dispute between the litigants.

Instrumentalism

A contrast to the party-centered method of rationalizing legal judgments that characterizes the purest form of corrective justice is an approach that is widespread in the American way of looking at the law. It goes under the name of "instrumentalism." Many, if not most, of your teachers will emphasize—or assume—an instrumentalist approach to the law. That is, they will assume that when one analyzes a legal dispute between particular individuals, one must consciously take into account the effects that a decision one way or another will have on society more generally.

Consider, for example, the question of whether a low-income purchaser who buys a consumer product—say, a color television set—at a very high interest rate should be able to avoid the sales contract on the theory that the contract is "unconscionable." Perhaps some courts would conclude that it would be "fair" to let the consumer get out of the contract—"fair" as between the parties. But under one instrumentalist approach to the problem, a court might reason that to free buyers from their contracts on a "fairness" basis would destabilize consumer markets for home electronics by increasing sellers' expenses. The result, in fact, might be to raise the overall price for color TVs, with particular harm to the poor consumers that the court presumably would be trying to protect by voiding the contract. The instrumentalism adopted by a court that refused to hold the contract unconscionable, which would take into account the larger policy implications of the case, would therefore yield a different result than at least a highly individualized form of corrective justice. This is not to say that the results produced by corrective justice and instrumentalism cannot coincide—only to indicate that sometimes the approaches will produce different outcomes.

Distributive Justice

Rather distinct from the concept of corrective justice is the idea of "distributive justice," which for present purposes we may define as a normative concept of how economic goods *should* be distributed, according to moral criteria such as the principle of equity. As has been the case in our prior discussions of parallel basic concepts, we do not mean to suggest these are airtight categories. However, American lawyers generally think of distributive justice as a job for a legislature. We allow Congress and state legislatures, within constitutional limits, to take from the rich and give to the poor—notably, through the tax system. A legislature literally *redistributes* wealth. If you think about it, you will recognize that frequently half the headlines on the front page of any newspaper deal with this issue in some form, especially when Congress or a state legislature is in session.

Of course, some judicial decisions may have redistributive effects. A decision that changes a general rule in pollution cases, with the practical result of favoring classes of people inconvenienced by discharges of toxic materials into air or water, might have substantial redistributive effects between industries and homeowners. Sometimes we allow judges to do this kind of distributive justice, but our system tends to be wary of allowing courts to serve as redistributive agencies. One way to express the general reason—an oversimplifying one, to be sure—is that we think of income distribution as a "political" rather than a "legal" matter. Given a theory that we should keep courts as "neutral" as possible, we try to steer them away from making "political," "redistributive" decisions—as much as possible. By contrast, we are much more prone to accept the idea that legislatures can transfer money from one class of people to another in the name of community ideas of fairness.

Courts and Legislatures Compared

A view widely shared by American lawyers and judges is that courts exist primarily to resolve disputes, employing relatively specific rules, while the main function of legislatures is to make relatively general rules for society, often arbitrating among the claims of competing interest groups.

Most students of the American legal system would agree, at some level of generality, that it is best for legislatures to resolve issues concerning moral choices that society must make, as well as questions about large-scale distribution of wealth. The argument is that elected representatives, representing the political will of the people, are best qualified to fight out big social questions.

By contrast, courts generally are deemed best able to deal with "interstitial" questions—issues that lie in the cracks within large questions of morality and within controversies about the distribution of resources between and among groups. Thus, generally speaking, no legislature has improved on the judicial administration of a standard of negligence that defines it as conduct that falls below a "reasonable standard of care." Part of the reason for this is that the concept of negligence must be applied to thousands of different situations, making it impossible for a legislature to fashion a code so precise that it would cover all those occurrences.

There are, however, areas of overlap between judicial and legislative roles as analysts traditionally distinguish them. Thus, a legislature might decide that a pattern of issues has arisen so often in litigation that it should adopt a specific rule to resolve those issues. Consider, for example, the question of whether the fact that a firm obeyed a governmental safety regulation should conclusively establish that it was not negligent with respect to injuries involving the regulated activity. Although sometimes a corporation might "really" be negligent even though it fulfilled the letter of a safety regulation, a legislature might decide that to save arguments about such questions that would otherwise arise in scores of cases, it should make a flat rule: one who obeys a safety regulation issued by an administrative agency may not be held negligent. A court could also announce such a rule on its own.

More dramatic examples of tensions in this zone of overlap—tensions less easily resolvable—appear in certain aspects of judicial review of legislation for constitutionality. Some of the most publicized modern illustrations are the decisions of the Supreme Court on segregation of public schools and on abortion. In holding that it was a denial of equal protection to segregate school children by race, the

Supreme Court effectively took over the resolution of a large social issue on which several state legislatures—presumably representing the majority will of their constituents—had made decisions that the Court considered unconstitutional. The Court's activity in this area has represented, at least in part, a moral choice.

The current jurisprudence on abortion also embodies a determination by the Court that decisions made by some state legislatures, involving strongly held moral premises, violate deeply rooted principles of constitutional policy. The continuing political argument on this set of issues confirms the degree of tension over the question of whether the legislature or the court is "supreme" in an area of disputed moral principles.

We offer these controversies simply to illustrate the sort of issue where you will encounter disputes about the appropriate domain of lawmaking for courts and legislatures.

Concepts of Judicial Administration

This Part presents a category of policy considerations that focuses on "judicial administration"—in simple terms, how courts run their own business. It is not immediately evident to many people beginning the study of law that an important factor in judicial decisionmaking is the impact of decisions on the court system itself. If one thinks about the point, however, it appears logical. Courts cost money. Courts are a last resort for dispute resolution, at least in our society. We want people to try to work out grievances among themselves, and we wish to use social resources to resolve disputes only if there is no other (peaceful) way to do that.

Requirement That There be a Dispute

One device that courts use to control their business is to require that there really is a dispute—you may hear of this idea in your Civil Procedure course in connection with the requirement that there be a "case or controversy" before the court. Courts use this concept to insist that the parties present a focused, present-time argument about a concrete issue. Judges say, in effect: Don't come to us because you think you are going to have an argument in the future. Don't ask us for "advisory opinions." We are not consultants; for that task, use a member of the clergy, or your friends and neighbors, or your psychotherapist, or even your lawyer. We, the courts, exist only to resolve actual disputes.

Discouraging Frivolous and Fraudulent Litigation

Judges try to insure that courts use their resources only for serious matters; they will not allow "frivolous litigation" and they are hostile to fraudulent claims.

When courts condemn "frivolous" lawsuits, they sometimes are announcing their belief that there is no ground in law for a claim and that the claimant's attorney should have known that. They are saying that an attorney is trying to build a legal structure where there is no foundation—either no legal rule that supports that claim or no facts to which to apply a valid legal rule. Sometimes they are saying that the plaintiff's allegations are too trivial for a court to take notice. For example, in rejecting a plaintiff's suit for mental suffering alleged to be caused by a bill collector's tactics, one court referred to "the 'wide door' which might be opened" if it allowed the claim, a door open "not only to fictitious claims, but to trivialities and mere bad manners."[4]

One should note that there can be a fine line between a frivolous claim and an argument to extend an established rule or to create a new one. Since under the rules of professional ethics, an attorney's representation of her client must be "zealous," courts that draw that line too restrictively may be accused of stifling that representation.

A different concern is outright fraud by litigants, including the fabrication of facts in order to present a complaint that cannot be dismissed. Besides being morally wrong, this kind of conduct can have destructive effects on people's perceptions of justice. A fraudulent claimant may, in effect, extort money from a defendant who settles because he would rather pay the "nuisance value" of a fraudulent suit than to fight it.

---

[4] Medlin v. Allied Inv. Co., 398 S.W.2d 270, 274 (Tenn. 1966).

Administrative Efficiency

Beyond wielding their axes against transparently frivolous or even fraudulent litigation, courts invoke other concerns of administrative efficiency to turn away disputes. They may tell a litigant that his or her grievance inspires their sympathy but that it just would be too costly, or otherwise too impractical, to do the judicial work necessary to resolve that claim.

An illustration appears in cases involving the shock felt by so-called "bystander witnesses"—people who are in the vicinity when someone else suffers physical injury in an accident. These "bystanders" do not sustain a physical contact themselves but they sue for mental suffering—or perhaps even physical consequences, such as a heart attack—because of the fright of seeing a terrible event.

Fifty people might observe an accident, and ten of them might suffer consequences from seeing the event that legitimately send them to the doctor. But courts try to minimize the chance that parades of claimants will come before them, especially when the alleged injuries are somewhat harder to pin down than the injuries typically caused by direct physical contact.

In order to sort out these cases, courts have created relatively limited categories of people who can recover for injuries suffered as "bystander witnesses." Principally, these will be relatives of the person who suffered a direct physical injury. In fact, courts probably will limit the persons who can recover to very near relatives—members of immediate families, or perhaps only spouses, or only parents if the victim of the physical injury is a minor.

What courts are saying to the other claimants, to whom they refuse recovery, is something like this: We do not deny that you may really have been hurt by witnessing this accident. But we cannot extend liability indefinitely. If we let you recover today because you saw your best friend hit by a car, maybe tomorrow we will have to hear a claim from someone who alleges serious psychological consequences from seeing a stranger struck by a car. Or perhaps we will have to entertain a suit by someone who was grief-stricken because he heard on the radio that his best friend was killed in an accident. To guard our dockets, and to keep from having to make super-fine distinctions, we must reject your suit and limit recovery to people who (1) actually witness accidents involving (2) near relatives. We are personally sympathetic, and we concede that your psychiatrist would testify that you have a real psychological injury from witnessing this accident. But as judges, we have to draw a line that keeps too many people from getting into court and that surely will keep the fanciful claims out of court.

Notice that this is a ruling as a matter of law. Even though the plaintiff might be able to prove as a fact that he or she has been emotionally injured by witnessing an accident, the court will not impose liability. Indeed, with a pleading that identified this kind of injury, it would grant a motion to dismiss the claim. The legal rule that limits the class of bystanders who can recover is a rule of law that cuts off some claims for factually "real" injuries.

Promoting Settlement

In their effort to achieve administrative efficiency, courts often focus on promoting settlement. Indeed, most of the federal courts of appeal assign a set percentage of cases to mandatory settlement conferences. The kinds of legal rules that courts choose will frequently affect the inclination of parties to settle cases, although sometimes that effect occurs in different ways. On some occasions, a relatively vague rule will promote settlement; because of their uncertainty about the law, parties will decide that it is better not to take a chance on the outcome of a trial. At other times, a rather precise rule will make clear the negotiating territory for settlement. Assume, for example, a negligence suit for loss of an arm. Assume further that a pattern of case law indicates that the state's appellate courts, in reviewing jury verdicts in personal injury cases, view the worth of an arm as $150,000. That will give both the plaintiff and defendant a basis for a settlement figure (which will be less than $150,000) that will save both sides the expense of a trial.

Obviously, a principal element of the judicial desire to have parties settle their cases rather than litigate them is that courts want to keep their own burdens manageable. But settlement does more than conserve judicial resources. It saves time, money, and often grief for litigants. Moreover, many people would invoke a philosophical reason for favoring settlement: it enhances community values to encourage disputants to work out their disagreements with each other.

Open Courts

Since you already have learned that lawyers have a comeback to almost any argument, you should not be surprised to find that there is a basic idea that competes with administrative efficiency. We can sum this up as the "open courts" idea. In fact, many state constitutions include what are sometimes labeled as "open courts" provisions, which seek to assure that the courts shall be "open" to citizen grievances.

Without trying even to capsulize the rather complicated bodies of law under those particular provisions, we simply note that, as a general matter, many judges are inclined to be relatively liberal about the kinds of complaints they will entertain. Of course, judges are sensitive to the pressure to control their caseloads—who wants to make more work for herself than she needs to? But American flags wave in the background when attorneys argue that courts should be more, rather than less, hospitable to complaints. If one really wanted to wrap the argument in patriotism, one might say that open courts are an important distinguishing feature between democracies and totalitarian governments. The point does not appear that boldly in the decisions, but the idea is there, in the judicial subconscious, when there is a close question about whether to let a case in the courthouse door. A related argument is that a relatively full judicial workload is a good rather than a bad thing, because questions of law have public content that deserves airing in a public forum.

Without resolving the competing arguments on these issues, we simply reiterate our main point in this Part. A fairly distinct set of policy concerns in the law relates to the administration of the justice system itself, rather than to the substantive aspects of particular rules. Of course, some of the policy rationales we discussed above under the heading of "jurisprudential concepts" relate rather directly to "judicial administration." For example, predictability in the law will not only help businesses plan their entrepreneurial lives, but will aid courts in controlling their dockets.

Limiting the Judge's Role: Self-restraint and Activism

As just one institution in the governance of human affairs, courts have a limited function in the overall scheme of law. We emphasize this point because many courses, especially first-year courses, tend to focus on judicial cases. That focus may implicitly convey the idea that judges can, or should, play more of a role than they do.

In fact, the ethic of judicial "self-restraint" is deeply embedded in the system. Most lawyers, whatever their political views, do not ordinarily view the role of judges as one of dispensing compassion, for example. At the least, judges tend to dress up humanitarian concerns in the garb of relatively neutral sounding reasons.

Part of this attitude arises from the idea, which we mentioned above, that the purposeful redistribution of wealth is generally a function for the legislature. This idea is a powerful one in the minds of American judges, even though judicial decisions may have the incidental effect of transferring wealth from one litigant to another. To exaggerate the point: There is a big difference between a court requiring A to pay B because A's negligence or breach of contract caused harm to B, which by general agreement is a legitimate judicial act, and a court requiring A to pay B because A has much more money than B, which by consensus is not a proper role for courts. Legislatures have a broader mandate. All legislators are elected representatives (though some judges are elected, too), and we have specifically invested legislatures with the power to make moral judgments about how resources are spread around. Of course, even that kind of legislative activity is subject to constitutional limitations, for example, by the prohibition in federal and state constitutions against taking property without due process of law.

Another set of concerns underlies the traditional, restrictive view of judicial limitations. We fear judges injecting their personal moralities into individual disputes. Some observers may stress that judges cannot avoid doing that. Most people, however, probably would agree at some level that our sense of fairness in decisionmaking resides in significant part in a belief of neutrality, or at least impartiality, in the decisionmaker. This view exerts a powerful drag against judges overtly making choices between or among competing moral ideas.

To be sure, the very idea of the common law, as well as our tradition of constitutional law, provides some room for "judicial activism." In the constitutional area, courts from time to time invalidate legislation—that is, they find statutes to be unconstitutional. This is a form of activism, because it consists of the court—often a non-elected court- –telling the legislature, which by definition represents the political will of the people, that it cannot have its way.

Courts dealing with common law cases also take activist roles on occasion, often without even thinking of themselves as being "activist." Notably, courts may formulate new theories of liability. Thus, in the area of contract law, courts have gone beyond requiring that both parties "sign on the dotted line," or even exchange oral promises. They have, for example, developed a doctrine that permits a party to sue for enforcement of a promise on which he took action in justifiable reliance, even though his response to the promise did not fulfill the traditional requirements for the making of contracts, "if injustice can be avoided only by enforcement of the promise."

In the area of tort law, courts occasionally create new doctrines that permit plaintiffs to recover damages in situations where the courts had not previously imposed liability. An example is the item of tort damages called loss of "consortium," which has been said to be shorthand for "sex, society and services." When courts began to award consortium damages, they gave them only to husbands. Eventually they began to approve such awards to wives, and also to permit analogous recoveries to children for loss of parental care and intangible relationships of affection. Each time a court takes a step like this, it arguably behaves in an "activist" manner.

Sometimes courts go beyond simply creating new categories of actions, an activity that itself will inevitably have the effect of transferring wealth from one party to another in particular disputes. In their bolder acts, courts occasionally will provide remedies that unavoidably redistribute resources between or among relatively broad classes of persons. For example, some federal trial courts have virtually taken over the management of certain state prisons, at least for a time, where prisoners significantly lacked basic protection and care. When courts do that, they effectively compel state governments—and thus taxpayers—to deliver more money for the benefit of prisoners.

It is beyond the scope of this book to describe the principles governing the scope and limits of judicial activity. For our present purposes, it is enough to note that under common law principles judges may adopt new liability doctrines, but also that most American judges have it bred in their bones that they should be very careful and selective about when they take steps that can be described as legislating. A good part of the reason lies in our sense that judges should not make broad social choices, nor should they impose their own moralities on litigants or society more generally. A deep root of that thinking lies in our fear of tyranny. Less dramatic, but still fundamental foundations for the constraints we place on judges lie in the doctrine of stare decisis, and in the idea that the law should be stable and certain so that ordinary people know what the law is and can rely on it.

10

Choices Among Policies

The competition among interests we have described in Chapter 8 gives rise to the need for decisionmakers to reconcile, or sometimes to choose among, the social policies described in Chapter 9 that underlie those interests. Those policies frequently clash with one another.

The Struggle Over the Goals of the Law

Judges always will be influenced by the pull of individual claims of justice in particular cases. It is useful to reiterate, however, that American courts, especially appellate courts, tend to be "instrumentalist"—that is, they look beyond the claims of the parties for individualized justice to the social implications of their decisions.

The law schools have provided important stimuli to the policy analysis of law in which courts now engage. In some law schools, students will find that there is quiet—sometimes not so quiet—warfare among their teachers about the primary goals of law and policy. Some teachers that have a law and economics slant, for example, will focus exclusively, or in very large part, on using the law to achieve efficiency. Others will suggest that the law should focus primarily on equity, or will emphasize redress of historic injustices. Some will say, or assume, that the power of the law lies in its ability to choose among different goals, and to accommodate several different sets of rationales and aspirations.

You ought to be aware that your teachers come to the law with intellectual baggage. Be prepared, as a pragmatic matter, to adapt to the particular prisms through which individual teachers view the law. This does not mean that you have to bow down to ideas that seem screwy to you. It does mean that sometimes you have to be alert to where a teacher is "coming from." Moreover, even if you violently disagree with a professor's views, you might learn something. At worst, you will learn that there is another side to issues on which you hold strong views. That realization, in itself, is part of a lawyer's equipment.

Justice-Oriented Concepts

What we have just said makes it evident that there is a wide spectrum of ideas that employ the terminology of "justice." Many people probably think of the problem of justice as basically involving issues concerning the distribution of wealth. That is certainly one version of justice, but its applications do not have to be as simple as the redistributive exploits of Robin Hood. A sophisticated set of ideas about justice in recent philosophical literature derives from the work of John Rawls. In very simplified form, the Rawls approach asks the decisionmaker to consider the distribution of goods that she would choose if she did not know, in advance, the place in life she would occupy at the time of the relevant litigation or social decision. How would you like wealth to be distributed if you did not know beforehand whether you would find yourself in the top third, the middle third, or the bottom third of the economic ladder?

Notions of ethics and morality tie in with the idea of justice. The justice orientation of some people, including some law professors, inclines towards equity; among other things, these people believe in relatively equal distributions of goods among the population. Others see that as a basically unethical position, because it fails to reward effort and the virtue that effort represents. Particularly if your past education has not focused on these questions, you may find that teachers who challenge you with them force you to do some of the hardest thinking you must do in law school.

Here are capsules of just a few of the positions that various teachers may advocate, sometimes out of conviction and sometimes to make you think.

The wealth maximizer will contend that the principal goal of law is to increase the total store of goods in society. One ethical justification draws on the practical assumption that the more goods are produced, the more they will be spread around, thus benefitting the poorer as well as the richer segments of the population.

The libertarian will argue that the law should strive to keep from intruding in people's affairs—to "stay off their backs"—letting them live their own lives and work out their own bargains among themselves so far as social peace allows. Libertarians frown on labor unions and civil rights laws. They will argue that union wages command more than an efficient share of the income of firms and that civil right laws, on balance, produce more discrimination than would exist without them. People who take the libertarian position also tend to oppose various kinds of regulatory regimes, such as the regulation of safety in the workplace. They would suggest that, in that particular environment, people should be able to decide whether they want to face a particular risk at a given wage without the interference of a paternalistic government.

Critical legal studies (CLS) scholars occupy a spectrum of positions about law, all of them critical of law as a tool of oppression. One thing that the so-called "crits" emphasize is that law is not neutral, but dominated by power. In their view, all law is political. They strongly oppose the notion that decisionmakers can be dispassionate and can put aside their experiences, perhaps even their emotions, when they decide disputes. Why does a particular judge construe labor legislation in favor of management, time after time? The roots of this judicial behavior, a "crit" might explain, lie partly in the fact that the judge was the child of a corporate manager, grew up with people in that stratum of society, and imbibed their assumptions about justice. Beyond that, many crits would insist that the judge is, at one level of consciousness or another, a tool of the managerial class.

Some practitioners of *critical race theory* carry this style of argument into legal controversies involving race, while sometimes criticizing CLS people for ignoring issues of race. Critical race commentators assert that the racial distinctiveness and cultural experiences of racial minorities have been ignored and marginalized by majority white society. They believe in the importance of race consciousness, and in using narratives to tell stories that reveal their experiences and underline the deficiencies of the law in not taking account of those experiences. They may insist, for example, that legislators and judges who are not African-American cannot understand the African-American experience and are thus unqualified to make laws dealing with racially sensitive subject matter or to preside over litigation in which that experience was a crucial factor. One example in the litigation area, illustrating how critical race theorists might question the use of white juries as well as judges, would be a civil suit by an African-American plaintiff alleging maltreatment by white arresting officers who continually uttered racial epithets.

Feminists are not a monolithic category. Their common enterprise, to be sure, involves the analysis of law through the prism of being female and, generally, includes a view of society as patriarchal. Early modern-day feminists—of the 1960s and 1970s—advocated equal opportunity in all areas to which the law applies, including employment, education, and family law. Some later feminists—the "difference feminists"—have instead advocated that women should be treated differently, that is, better, in order to compensate for past disadvantages and to obtain meaningful equality. An even later strand of feminist thinking has come to emphasize women's individually different experiences. Like critical race theorists, these feminists use narratives and storytelling to manifest their diverse experiences and to demonstrate the unresponsiveness of the law.

Many current issues divide those who call themselves feminists. The issue of surrogate motherhood[2] provides an example of the diversity of points of view. Some feminists oppose surrogacy but others applaud it as an exercise of reproductive choice. Those who argue against the practice see it as a form of slavery of women, a patriarchal and medical conspiracy to control women's bodies. They

---

[2] The term surrogate mother refers to a woman who contracts, usually with a childless married couple, to carry a baby and then give the baby to the couple for adoption. Typically, the baby is conceived by artificial insemination of the surrogate with the sperm of the contracting male.

criticize surrogacy as harmful to society, both as promoting baby selling and as degrading to the individual surrogate, whom they label "a rented womb." By sharp contrast, feminists who favor surrogacy argue that to protect women from entering into contracts is itself degrading and paternalistic.

At the same time, one should note that feminists will generally come together on certain ideas. You will not find any feminists laughing about the idea that negligence law has "never spoken of the reasonable woman." In fact, you probably will find few torts teachers—feminists or not—who invoke that idea, which used to be considered good humor, even a staple of some teachers' classroom instruction. To take an even clearer example, the impact of feminism has made it clear that rape is not amusing. It may surprise you to learn that this was not necessarily the case in criminal law classes less than a generation ago.

Some Basic Economic Ideas

Many law professors introduce principles of microeconomics into their classes in order to help to explain the law, or in some cases to challenge it. Those teachers who employ economic theory will go much deeper than we do here. We aim to present, for reference, a convenient set of capsulized ideas that recur in the application of economic ideas to law. If you become weary of the details of economic analysis—the leaves on individual trees in the economic forest, so to speak—you may want to refer to this summary as a way of viewing the whole forest.

Scarcity, Prices and Demand; the "Free Lunch"

Economic analysis generally proceeds on the premise that goods—which include tangible items, documents that represent rights to things, and services—are scarce. This principle covers automobiles, stereo equipment, law school coursebooks, certificates of deposit, and visits to the dentist. People, who are generally acquisitive, indicate the strength of their desire to possess a good by how much they are willing to pay for it.

A related concept is that there is a close relationship between the price of a good and the demand for it. Generally, as the price of a good increases, there will be a decrease in the number of units of that good that people will purchase. Conversely, when a producer lowers the price of a good, people will buy more of it. The conventional economic chart of this phenomenon, which will generally match up with your intuition, is called the "negatively sloped demand curve."

You have probably heard the phrase that "There is no such thing as a free lunch." Sometimes there may well be, but economic theory teaches us that, one way or another, we usually wind up paying a price for a good. Your college alumni office may invite you to a buffet supper party at which you do not have to pay for food or drink. If you value your minutes and hours, however, you may put a price on your own expenditure of time when you have to stand and listen to the inevitable fund-raising appeal. Thus, you have "paid" for supper.

A topical example is the use by law students of electronic research services—WESTLAW and LEXIS. To superficial appearances, these come free to you. But the library's contract with the providers of these data bases inevitably will find its way into the cost of your tuition.

Undoubtedly, this kind of analysis can get rather tortured. It will lead you into thinking that if a good friend buys you lunch, it is not out of the goodness of his or her heart, or "simple friendship," but because he or she wants something. However far you want to take this approach, the main point to remember is that there is often something to the idea that free lunches are not truly free.

Free Markets

The economic theory presented in law school classes generally assumes free markets, or at least begins with a model of unregulated markets in which people are free to sell and buy goods and services at mutually agreed prices. Two basic ideas tied in with markets are those of shopping ("searching") and bargaining. It is assumed that, within the limits of their resources, and given competing demands on those resources, consumers will shop for the goods that best fulfill their needs and, where it is possible to make deals with sellers, will bargain over price and other features of goods and services. Another basic concept assumes the existence of competition (except, of course, where there is none, as in the case of monopolies).

The idea of shopping, or searching, shows the importance of *information* in markets. In fact, if you have not studied economics, it is very useful to focus on the fact that information is not costless. You might buy a CD player for $150 at store X, not knowing that store Y, in easy walking distance, sells the same device for $117.50. Had you only known, you might say; but it would take some searching to acquire the information. Information, then, like the CD player itself, is a costly economic good.

If you have not had training in economic theory, you may get frustrated, from time to time, with certain assumptions that economics-oriented professors make about the nature of markets. You may think it is somewhat silly to talk about bargaining for price on a can of supermarket tomatoes, for example. However, the fact is that because you—and other consumers—are free to shop, all of you together engage in a masked form of bargaining about price with all sellers of canned tomatoes. Those sellers, because of competition, are always pricing their goods with an eye to what consumers are willing to pay, and to the level at which they think their competitors will set prices.

Our basic point is that you should treat the theoretical assumptions you encounter about markets in the same way you should treat the conventional use of legal hypotheticals. Do not be unduly quarrelsome, get used to economic theory, and make it your servant.

Efficiency

There are several basic definitions of efficiency, and volumes of variations. We begin by propounding one simple idea: The quest for economic efficiency involves, among other things, the effort to put resources to their most socially valued use. That is a neutral (some might think cold-blooded) concept. It does not have to do with fairness,[3] or ethics, or morality. The question is only what the people

---

[3] We discuss the concept of fairness below, at pages 125-127.

in a given economy, taken together, declare with their dollars (or pounds or yen) is most valuable to them.

This definition of efficiency implies that the efficient solution may not necessarily be the fair solution. If a newly built factory pollutes the air over several homeowners' dwellings, it may violate some people's sense of justice. Efficiency-oriented economists will suggest, however, that if we are to take seriously the idea of putting resources to their best use, a flourishing factory that in effect uses a few homes as a sink for its pollution may be the most efficient use of the air over those homes. Moreover, if one thinks in terms of comparing benefits and costs, one may decide that consumers of the factory's products will value those products highly enough that the economic contribution of the factory to society will far outweigh the annoyance, and perhaps even the ill health, that the pollution causes to a few homeowners.

Well and good, you may say, but those homeowners were there first. Some of their properties have been in their families for generations. The efficiency-oriented economist might respond, "I understand your concern, but you are talking about fairness and even sentimentality, not efficiency." The relevant point is that efficiency, on the one hand, and fairness in wealth distribution or in the allocation of resources, on the other hand, are distinct concepts. You may resist this idea. However, you should understand that efficiency-oriented economists do not necessarily contend that one should not be concerned about fairness. They observe, however, that if what one truly wants is efficiency—and, perhaps the greatest good for the greatest number—the efficient solution may be unfair for some people. They also point out that when disputing parties offer contradictory versions of fairness, efficiency analysis will help us to see how much it will cost to achieve one brand of fairness or another.

Note, at the same time, that one may introduce some wrinkles in this form of analysis. Some of these variations have to do with the question of how one values both resources and costs. For example, one might put a value on the good health of the homeowners that outweighs the value of the pollution-causing factory. Or, the homeowners might contend that a court should recognize a theory of social value beyond that represented by market prices. They might argue, for example, that the value of having stable communities that last for generations is worth as much in an intangible sense as the factory's production is worth at market prices. Alternatively, they might secure some experts in historic preservation to testify about the benefits society would realize from preserving their homes as historic places. They might also refer to such intangible costs as the increased tension that the pollution inflicts on their everyday lives and their relationships, the fact that their children cannot play outside after school, and the general destruction of community values. Some people might value those costs at more than the production of the factory, which would suggest that the factory should be liable even if the sole standard for liability is inefficient conduct. These might be hard arguments to sell to many economists, but we are just trying to point out that there is some flexibility in definitions of value and cost. The practical effect of valuing intangibles at significant levels might be to raise the cost of pollution to a level where the imposition of liability on the polluter would be judged efficient, as well as fair.

Property Rights

A concept with crucial linkages to economic analysis of law, and particularly to questions of efficient resource allocation, is that of property rights. How do we define what a property right is, and how do we determine when someone has one, to whom the right should be assigned, and what the consequences are of having such a right? Consider the different sorts of legal problems where these issues may prove fundamental.

- Mr. A begins openly occupying a piece of land to which Ms. B had title, and stays there for 15 years, during which Ms. B never shows up or demonstrates any attachment to the land. The doctrine of "adverse possession" may transfer the property right to Mr. A.
- A coal-fired railroad engine gives off sparks that cause fires on farmland that borders the tracks. Should the farmers be able to recover damages from the railroad company? Is

there only one relevant "property right"—that of the farmers to the undisturbed agricultural use of their land? Or is there a countervailing "property right"—that of the railroad to pursue its lawful business of carrying passengers and freight?

- The X Company drills for petroleum in coastal waters, causing an oil spill that kills a large number of fish in fishing grounds that have consistently yielded profits to Y, a fisherman. Can Y be said to have a sufficient "property right" in fish that swim in the open sea to sue X Company for the loss of his profits?

- A county e tends the runways of a county-owned airport to accommodate bigger jets, which cause much more noise over a larger area than previously was bothered by jet noise. If it does not compensate the homeowners whose property is newly affected, will the county be "taking" private property without just compensation, which is prohibited by the Fifth Amendment to the Constitution?

- The owner of a shopping mall wishes to keep political groups from handing out leaflets to customers on the premises. Can the owner do so without violating the First Amendment?

- A state government wants to force owners of oceanfront property to give up strips of land so that members of the public can reach the beach. If it did so without paying for the strips of land, would it be unconstitutionally "taking" private property?

These few examples will give you a flavor of the ways in which the definition—and assignment—of property rights may affect the results in cases in diverse areas of the law. Among other things, they introduce the fact that the assignment of property rights often will be critical to the determination of whether an application of a legal rule is efficient or not. They also underline the importance of the distinction between private property and public property, and the need for law to play a role in resolving disputes about the limits of both.

Incentives and Disincentives

An important prism through which to view both law and economics is that of incentives. Economists put special stock in incentive effects for their own professional purposes, and sometimes devise rather technical measures for them. You, however, can go a long way in *legal* analysis by using your common sense about the tendency of particular legal rules to influence behavior.

A rather fundamental point is that incentives can be either positive or negative. Some rules will inspire people to more intense levels of certain kinds of activity. Others will provide disincentives—they will discourage particular types of behavior.

Consider, for example, the rule of contract law that presumes that one who signs a contract has read the document. The tendency of this rule is clear: it creates an incentive to read contracts, because it tells people who are preparing to make an agreement that there will be no profit in later claiming that they did not read what they signed. Almost every rule of law, from the simplest to the most complicated, may be argued to have incentive effects.

An illustration of a rule that creates disincentives would be a rule that permits a court to award punitive damages for fraud. Such an award would be added to damages that give the plaintiff the difference between what he has received in a transaction and what he would have received if the bargain had been as the defendant represented. The so-called "benefit of the bargain" rule is a traditional measure of contract damages. The threat of having to pay an award that not only reflects the economic loss caused by a fraud (the lost benefit of the bargain), but adds a sum for the defendant's ethical transgression (the punitive damages), is likely to make people think more than twice about telling lies concerning the value of their goods.

Lawyers will often argue about the factual basis for assumptions concerning the incentive effects of rules. For example, an empirical disagreement may arise about whether one party to a fight to which both parties assented should be able to recover damages from the other for injuries that the other inflicted. Those who argue that there should be liability declare that such a rule will discourage fighting, since the prospect of having to pay damages to an opponent will make people much more cautious about engaging in brawls. The people who argue there should be no liability, however, contend that if one knows that he will not be able to recover for injuries that he himself suffers in a fight, he will be discouraged from slugging it out. Thus, both sides say that the rule that favors them will deter fighting.

This problem, featuring diametrically opposed assertions about the effects of yes-and-no rules on behavior, presents a good example of the sort of issue concerning incentive effects on which there is not likely to be solid social science research. For practicing lawyers, such an issue would leave a lot of room for effective advocacy that appeals to the experience and intuition of the judge or jury. The illustration also demonstrates to the law student that often there is plenty of room for plausible-sounding arguments on both sides about the incentive effects of particular rules.

Externalities

A key concept in economic theory related to law is that of the "externality." This section seeks to provide a concise description of the "externality" idea, and also to show you how both lawyers and economists can use it as a tool of argument.

We mostly tend to think of externalities as being negative effects from the conduct of others. An obvious example is smokestack pollution from a factory that causes illness in persons who live nearby. Another pretty clear example is A's loud stereo noise that keeps B from reading this book. A somewhat subtler illustration appears in the argument that a particular kind of gas tank design on a car is associated with an unacceptably high degree of injury to passengers when collisions occur. In suing on the basis that the design is "defective," a person burned in a collision-triggered explosion would in effect claim that his injuries were "externalities" of the design.

An argument that goes along with the concept of externalities is that those who cause them should have to "internalize the externalities." In plain English, or plain law, this means that the polluter should have to pay for illnesses caused by his pollution, or that the car maker should have to compensate those injured by the gas tank design. The notion is that the damages award will force the firm to internalize the costs rather than imposing them on others.

When lawyers and economists play games with the "externalities" idea, it will make a lot of difference how one describes whose ox is being gored. For example, in the stereo case above, A might claim that it is B's hypersensitivity to sound, rather than A's playing of her music, that is the cause of B's complaint. Therefore, A would argue that there is no externality attributable to her. Perhaps even the smokestack owner would claim that whatever externality there is arises from the presence of the nearby residents, whose sensitivity to smoke impinges on his ability to produce useful goods in his factory. That argument would have particular force if the residents built their houses after the factory had started production.

A further twist is the concept of the "positive externality." If I have excellent flower beds in my garden, that confers an esthetic benefit on my neighbor. Indeed, since my neighbor provides neither fertilizer, seed, nor labor to my garden, she may be said to be a "free rider" on the positive externality of my flowers. She benefits from the flower beds without contributing to them.[4]

Of course, a firm or person might generate negative and positive externalities at the same time. If a hamburger stand starts up business next door to me, its negative externalities include loud crowds and people dropping wrappers on my lawn. Its positive externalities for me, if I like hamburgers, would include an increased ability to secure a quick and tasty dinner. How would you describe the cooking odors? For strict vegetarians who could not stand anything connected with the cooking of meat, the odors always would be negative externalities. For those who like the smell of frying burgers, they would be positive. In fact, the same hamburger lover might consider cooking odors to be positive externalities at dinner time and negative externalities when they waft through his window late at night.

The Moral Hazard

A thread that runs through economic analysis of law is the concept of moral hazard. For our present purposes, we may describe a moral hazard as a state of affairs that creates incentives for people to behave

---

[4] See pages 127-128 below for a discussion of "free riders."

in inefficient, or even criminal, ways that will throw the losses associated with that conduct onto others. The law frowns on moral hazards. Consider these examples.

- A federal insurance program permits people to get insurance for homes that they build in areas with high risks of flooding. The moral hazard is that the taxpayer will have to pay for the improvidence of the insured homeowners.
- A rule of tort law eliminates the ability of defendants to plead that plaintiffs have themselves been careless with respect to the risks that injured them. The moral hazard is that defendants, and ultimately the people who use their goods and services, will have to pay the price of plaintiffs' failure to take care for their own safety. (Some people may consider this a rather theoretical concern.)
- An insurance company issues a life insurance policy on the life of A to B, a person with no family or business relation to A and no financial dependence on A's life continuing. B murders A for the insurance money. The issuance of the policy created the moral hazard of the murder, because B had no stake in A continuing to live and a positive incentive to end A's life.

The Coase Theorem

In the course of their studies, many law students will encounter an idea called "the Coase theorem." This idea, much used by professors who like to do economic analysis of law, takes its name from a Nobel Prize-winning economist, Ronald Coase. For those who have not studied economics, it may seem opposed to intuition. We suggest, however, that you consider it for its potential power to shed light on legal problems.

Coase argued that when two parties interact with a result that ordinary people would characterize as one causing injury to the other, it will make no difference to "resource allocation"—essentially to efficiency—who will have to bear the cost. At least, this will be so if there are no "transaction costs"—if the parties could work out deals and bargains concerning the behavior at issue without expense. In dealing with this form of analysis, you must keep in mind the assumption that in the absence of transaction costs, parties in a free market will bargain to efficient results. It is also important to understand that Coase himself understood very well that transaction costs permeate most of life. In fact, he spent a significant part of the article in which he invented his "theorem" explaining the potential implications of transaction costs for legal rules.[5]

Coase's principal example[6] concerned a rancher's cattle trespassing on the crops of his farmer neighbor. Coase premised that in a purely marketplace setting the farmer and the rancher would bargain out the issues that would inevitably arise. If, for example, the law refused to impose liability for crop damage on the rancher, the farmer would pay a "bribe" to the rancher to get him to decrease the size of his herd, which would effectively reduce the loss to the farmer's crops. Coase concluded that whether the law imposed liability on the rancher or let the loss remain on the farmer, the *economic* outcome would be the same. Here is the reasoning that applies to this admittedly pristine example: If the law let the loss stay with the farmer, he would bribe the rancher to reduce his herd. If the law imposed liability on the rancher, he would reduce his herd. Either way, the herd would be reduced, and the result would be efficient, given the amounts that consumers in the broader world are prepared to pay for beef and corn.

Your response may be that if the court lets the loss stay with the farmer, this seems a miserably unfair result, whether it is efficient or not. The farmer will be out of pocket because of the rancher's trespassing cattle. You might say, indeed, that this sounds like a classic example of an "externality." The answer of efficiency analysis to this criticism is one that we provided in an earlier section: Efficiency and fair wealth distribution are quite separate things, even though on some happy occasions they may coincide. Your own instinct may favor achieving a "fair" result by imposing liability on the rancher. However, you should understand that, under the Coase theorem, if there are no transaction costs, it would make no difference to resource allocation—i.e., "efficiency"— whichever way courts

---

[5] We will focus on transaction costs at pages 124-125 below.

[6] Ronald Coase, The Problem of Social Cost, 3 J.L. & Econ. 1 (1960).

decide the liability issue. Let us be clear, to the point of repetition. Efficiency-oriented economists do not necessarily say you should not adopt fairness as your principal goal. Their invocation of the Coase theorem simply emphasizes that if what you really desire is efficiency, you should not allow fairness-oriented sentiments to obscure what may be efficient rules.

Transaction Costs

Volumes have been written about the Coase theorem, and we have given you just a primer. But even this primer would be incomplete if we did not introduce the major qualification of the theorem—the assumption that there are no "transaction costs." The reason that Coase could assume that there were no transaction costs in his hypothetical of the cattle and the crops is that the rancher and the farmer didn't need lawyers or even fax machines to discuss their dispute. All they had to do was bargain face to face amidst the marauding livestock and the corn. But once one plugs in items like the cost of getting information and the cost of negotiation, a new set of questions arises.

One useful way to describe this set of issues—and indeed a lot of law and economics problems—is to say that an important task of rulemakers is to search for the party who is in the best position to minimize relevant costs—the "least cost avoider." Consider, for example, a case involving a factory that pollutes water in a stream that serves ten thousand homeowners. Courts may reason in such a case that it is more efficient to have a rule that requires the factory to use pollution control devices than one that effectively forces the homeowners to band together to bribe the factory owner. The theory is that it would be prohibitively expensive for the homeowners to organize themselves to put together a pot of bribe money; this is a transaction cost that is inefficiently high. In addition, many homeowners might try to ride the coattails of those who are doing the work on the issue. They would free ride—take advantage, without bearing any of the negotiating cost themselves—on the efforts of the more energetic homeowners to stop the pollution.[7]

---

[7] See pages 127-128 on "free riders."

One could turn the argument around, of course. One could focus on the expense to which the factory owner would be put to locate and bribe several thousand homeowners to let him keep polluting. And one could spin out the argument, contending that it would be cheaper for the homeowners to acquire filtration devices to combat the pollution, or perhaps even to move, than to make the factory owner locate them and bribe them or to install pollution control devices. The main point is that acquiring information and engaging in the transactions that are necessary to complex agreements are often costly. That is why "transaction costs," and more generally the search for the lowest cost avoider, represent an important part of economic analysis of law.

Fairness, Overreaching and Coercion

Even a highly professional analysis of the efficiency of legal rules will not solve every case—perhaps not most cases. Ideas of fairness continually influence the judicial mind, sometimes at a subconscious level, and persuade courts to reach what they consider fair outcomes. Of course, the concept of fairness may mean very different things to different people, and competing concepts of fairness will often lead the people who hold them to arrive at opposite results in concrete cases. This section deals with a few of the meanings that people give most frequently to the term. As a general matter, it is a word that should put your mind on critical alert. When someone says she wants only to be fair, you automatically should ask, "What do you mean, 'fair'?"

One important meaning of fairness relates to the way that resources are spread among individuals. As we suggested above, judges have been inculcated with the idea that the equitable distribution of wealth, or even of risky circumstances of life, is pretty much a subject for the legislature, for example, through rates of taxation or occupational safety legislation. Yet, judicial decisions often reflect concerns with achieving fairness between litigants.

Another meaning of fairness has to do with perceived inequities in power relationships. Some cases that especially appeal to courts on fairness grounds involve plaintiffs who appear very vulnerable in the particular circumstances, and perhaps defendants who seem to be overreaching. There is, indeed, controversy about how far courts should go to redress perceived imbalances in bargaining power.

In the area of contracts for the sale of consumer goods, for example, theoretical controversy exists about whether courts should declare certain contractual terms to be "unconscionable"—in effect, so unfair that they should not be enforced. The Uniform Commercial Code permits courts to refuse enforcement to contracts that they find to be unconscionable. However, the reason that some people react uncomfortably to the unconscionability doctrine is that they think it is hard to find a principled stopping place for that line of argument. If I say that Company A is unfairly "taking advantage of" Consumer B because Company A is a wealthy business and Consumer B is poor and uneducated, then may it not present a philosophical problem to allow that consumer to make contracts at all? Moreover, would not placing such a limit on the ability to contract make society a lot less free than it is? Could it have overall effects that harm more people than the unconscionability doctrine aids? For example, might it not discourage merchants from opening stores in economically depressed neighborhoods, because of fear that courts will find their sales practices to be unconscionable in those settings? This is how the arguments run.

There are, to be sure, some situations in which even the most efficiency-focused economists will say that they will not tolerate the use of economic power. For these situations, we employ concepts like coercion and extortion. A classic analogy for coercion—which goes well beyond the use of economic power— is the robber putting his gun to the citizen's head: "Your money or your life."

There is no freedom in that "transaction"— a lot less freedom, even, than the case in which someone with a sixth grade education buys a television set from Company A for twice the price charged by Company X, just a few blocks away. We make the armed robber's conduct a crime, but we are a lot less sure about calling it illegal to charge prices that are "too high." We are hesitant to have the law condemn that conduct even though most people would be willing to concede that there is not much "freedom" for buyers when there is no Company X nearby and the buyer lacks transportation to take her to a place where price competition exists.

Now suppose that someone says that he will provide you "protection" against your tires being slashed by "vandals," when you both know perfectly well that if you do not pay up, it is he who will do the slashing. Is that "extortion"?

Or suppose someone builds a factory that does not make automobiles, or air-conditioners, or cardboard boxes. The factory makes only smoke, and it does so only in order to force surrounding landowners to pay the factory owner not to make smoke. Is that extortion? After all, the factory owner is producing something—smoke!

Among other things, these examples highlight the fact that at some point, overreaching—and "unfair" conduct generally—may also become inefficient. One way to define that point is to say that it occurs where the market is no longer free. Armed robbery, at least, is an unambiguous example of an unfree exchange.

Free Riders

As we indicated above, a favorite target of economic criticism related to legal policy is the "free rider" problem. Often, when a group of people desire a particular outcome, a small number of them will work creatively to achieve that good. Their work will produce benefits that all the others in the group will realize without contributing to the effort of the activists. Let us say that it would be a great advantage to a village, in which 100 people live, to build a road to the next village. Working in their spare time, 50 village members do the plowing, scraping and surfacing to build the road. All 100 villagers, however, will use the road to their benefit, both through commerce and visits with relatives and friends. The 50 who did not help are "free riders." One way to deal with this problem would be to charge for use of the road, perhaps giving the volunteers a discount or a free pass. An analogous situation occurs in another setting when associations for the preservation of wilderness areas succeed with lobbying campaigns that benefit many non-members. The non-members are free riders, but it may not be so easy to charge them their fair, or efficient, share of the benefits produced by the association.

The Prisoner's Dilemma

A parallel concept that speaks to the problem of reconciling isolated individual incentives is that of "the prisoner's dilemma." The basic idea is familiar to anyone who has seen a cop show on television where two people, suspected of participation in a serious crime, face grillings in separate interrogation rooms. The prisoner's dilemma arises from the fact that one suspect does not know what the other suspect is saying.

The way that the "prisoner's dilemma" is usually presented in academic treatments is this: The prosecutor wants to convict both prisoners at the maximum sentence for the crime—say ten years—but has evidence to convict each only of a lesser crime that carries a one-year sentence. The only way that the prosecutor can get a conviction at the ten-year maximum is to extract a confession from one prisoner that the other did the deed. The prosecutor begins by offering a deal for a somewhat lesser sentence (five years) to either prisoner who confesses. He follows up by promising that he will make the sentence lighter still (two years) if either prisoner is the first to confess and will testify against the other, with a rather heavy sentence (seven years) for the other if he later confesses and tries to inculpate the first confessor. If both prisoners stay silent, the worst that can happen to them is that each will receive the one-year sentence on the lesser charge.

In this situation, silence would be the strategy with the least joint risk to both prisoners, since the worst it would bring them is a sentence of one year apiece. But since the prisoners cannot communicate, the incentive for each would be to quickly confess and inculpate the other. If one beats the other in confessing, it will result in a two-year sentence for the confessor and a seven-year one for the later confessor. If they both confess at the same time, they will each get five years. Their motivation to take a step that will be more costly than silence is that each will fear that the other will confess more than each will think that the other will join in stonewalling.

Thus, the following dilemma exists: Each would have gotten only a one-year sentence if they could have conferred and been rational about their choice (silence). But they might well wind up with five-year sentences for each (if they confess at the same time), and the best either can do is a two-year sentence while the other gets seven (if both confess but one confesses first).

The power of the prisoner's dilemma metaphor is that it describes problems often faced by free people as well. A principal problem of this sort is that people in the pursuit of their narrowly defined self-interest may wind up making deals that are actually inferior to the bargains that could be made if they got together with others in roughly the same position and worked out an arrangement advantageous to all. This is where basic efficiency theory and the game theory represented by the prisoner's dilemma come together to favor cooperation. Of course, important antidotes for the prisoner's dilemma are the possession of information and the freedom to act on that information.

Our general point is that under the roof of economic theory, there is plenty of room for people to blunt their competitive instincts and work for a goal that includes the welfare of others. However, just because lawyers are always complicating things, we have to add that if business competitors go too far in cooperating between or among themselves, they may be guilty of an antitrust violation. That would be the case, for example, when companies selling competing products agree to keep their prices at the same high level, with the result that consumers pay more than the price that would exist if the cooperating "competitors" were really "competing." In any event, part of your law study will involve the question of how to balance competition and cooperation.

The Tragedy of the Commons

The "tragedy of the commons" is another idea that draws on the potential tension between individual self-interest and cooperation. This concept has been used to support the case for assigning property rights to private owners rather than to the public. A simple form of the argument may appeal to your intuition. I have a stake in a tidy lawn, and I will keep it clipped. I have a property right in "my" lawn. But if I share a big backyard with three other people, and none of us individually owns it, it is rather likely that that parcel of land—a "commons" that belongs to everyone in general but no one in particular—will get weedy. None of us has sufficient incentive to keep it up. And if one of us does, the others will be free riders. This arguably is unfair, as well as inefficient.

If you would like to tease yourself, though, assume that the real property involved is not a patch of land that lies among four homes, but the Grand Canyon. Would you think that turning that piece of real estate over to a private corporation would keep it free of candy wrappers and optimally pristine? Or would government better serve the common enterprise? Can people cooperate best in preserving natural wonders through the medium of private marketeers? Or would it be less of a "tragedy" for the Government to operate that particularly grand "commons"?

A Note on Selfishness

An issue that underlies many of the policy clashes that you will confront in law classes concerns the assumptions we make about self-interest. One strong position is that, as a matter of describing the world as it is, the rewards of life go to the self-interested. In this view, which comes from sociobiology, our genes seek to maximize their own survival and, by extension, so do we. As a principal promoter of the idea of "the selfish gene" put it, "[t]he universe that we observe has precisely the properties we should expect if there is, at bottom, no design, no purpose, no evil and no good, nothing but pitiless indifference."[8]

A contrasting position stresses the competing idea of altruism. It invokes conduct that most people would consider unselfish, for example, the behavior of people who risk their lives to save others without "expect[ing] or consider[ing] rewards for their acts."[9] You can imagine the sorts of arguments that would occur between defenders of an unvarnished selfishness model and advocates of altruism.

Why do soldiers brave death to rescue a stranded comrade? Some might contend that the rescuers think that the chances of their own

[8] Richard Dawkins, God's Utility Function, 273 *Scientific American* No. 5, 80 at 85 (November 1995).
[9] Kristen Monroe, Michael Barton and Ute Klingemann, Altruism and the Theory of Rational Choice: Rescuers of Jews in Nazi Europe, 101 *Ethics* 103, 120 (1990).

survival will be heightened because of the skills that even a wounded soldier would contribute to the group. Somewhere in the subconscious of the rescuing soldiers, these commentators would insist, is a selfish motive.

There are intermediate positions. Each soldier might reason that if he did not participate in a rescue, the other members of the squad would not be likely to rescue him if he got into a similar spot. We could certainly discern selfishness in that motivation. Or perhaps the members of the squad would decide that if they do not rescue the wounded soldier, morale will drop and their general chances of survival would be diminished.[10]

Sociobiologists would themselves suggest that a soldier would aid in the rescue, perhaps without thinking through costs and benefits in a refined way, because impulses of that sort are embedded in the genes through generations of living in social environments. This response, labelled "reciprocal altruism," is behavior by one person that benefits another on the assumption that someone will provide a benefit in the future to the "altruist" or someone who is genetically related to him. Yet we would not want to ignore the quite different argument that the real reason that people rescue others is because of a learned, ingrained moral sense that it is right to do so and perhaps even that it would be wrong not to do so.

This brief summary just illustrates how each person who engaged in this argument would criticize the others. We seek only to sensitize you to the question of what role selfishness actually plays in human activity, and how the law should respond.

***

Which views will your professors hold on justice, morality, and ethics? We are inclined to say that you will be lucky if your little platoon of teachers each year presents different points of view on the law. That would broaden your education.

We think you will be luckier still if those teachers who hold strong points of view are open to competing arguments. You will have to get a feel for this in particular classes. You will, frankly, have to

---

[10] Some people would say that this is simply an attempt to maximize the number of lives saved within the squad. Here, we will not go more deeply into the disagreements that occur between advocates of the "selfish gene" hypothesis and "efficiency maximizers."

estimate how open individual teachers will be to your presentation of ideas that oppose their own, in class or on examinations. We hope they would be disposed to consider opposing ideas, but you will have to play the game according to your sense of your teacher's hospitality to arguments against his or her own position.

How Argument Sharpens the Mind: Two Examples

If may be useful to provide a couple of examples of how arguments about fundamental beliefs and policy rationales may fly back and forth in discussions about legal issues—even in your own mind. First, suppose that you confront a case in which a buyer claims that a seller did not disclose some crucial information about the product or service that she was selling, which she easily could have done.

> 1) Your first tentative reaction might be that there should be very little, if any, room for fraud claims by those who claim that they were lured into purchases by nondisclosures of important information. You might rationalize this reaction on the ground that the prizes in all markets should go to people who have themselves acquired pertinent information about goods and services, and that providing fraud remedies for nondisclosure is actually unethical because it would reward people who did not have the foresight or energy to secure relevant information.
>
> 2) Then you might start thinking about a competing set of ethical principles, one that suggests that everyone should be regarded as having an equal opportunity to life's goods. You might conclude that in sales transactions, one of the most important of those goods is information, and you might then tentatively decide that it is morally unfair for someone to withhold knowledge crucial to a purchase, when she could disclose it with no more effort than uttering a sentence.

3) Then you might think further that to impose a remedy for fraud will have a dulling effect on purchasers' minds, when what you want to encourage is a sharpening of the wits. You might reason that alert buyers make for competitive market-places, which benefits everyone in the end.

4) Having swung back to a position that opposes a vigorous law of fraud, you might then consider the fact that sometimes people who possess crucial information are in that position not because they sweated to obtain it, but because they were lucky. And you might decide that the law should not reward luck, because then the law would sound like a lottery.

5) If you really wanted to torment yourself, though, you might consider a statement that Louis Pasteur is said to have made: "Chance favors the prepared mind." As applied in this case, that would mean that most times that we call people lucky because they came across important information, it was not because of random luck but because they had worked hard to put themselves in a position where the information would come to them. And you would tilt back to an outcome in favor of the silent seller.

6) Of course, there still might be a part of your mind that hung onto a purely egalitarian idea—that, as much as possible, the law should even up goods (including information) among people. Asked what the justification was for that position, that part of you might respond that it is simply a "first principle" that we treat people equally.

This example, a kind of ping-pong game of arguments, simply underlines the fact that most of us carry around several different positions in our minds—positions that will be reflected, in sometimes exaggerated ways, in the stances that different professors take in the classroom. As you come to understand that the law requires people to reason through competing arguments and choose the best ones, your own wits will in fact become sharper, and your legal education will be on its way.

A second illustration of the struggle over basic premises comes from the law of torts. Torts teachers who are devotees of economic theory may argue that there is only one worthy instrumentalist goal for tort law: to achieve efficient levels of deterrence. Others will suggest that the primary function of tort law is to require compensation for injuries caused by activities that are judged too risky on a social scale that uses broader measures than efficiency, an approach that sometimes may produce brands of justice that are inefficient from a technical economic viewpoint. Still another group of professors will argue that tort law should principally strive to do individual justice between the parties, without reference to considerations of social policy.

Our example, which highlights several differences in approach, involves a maker of children's toys that sells a million units of a particular product per year. It would cost 30 cents more per unit each year to achieve complete safety in a feature of the product that is known to cause a $200,000 injury to one child per year.

- One might argue that it would be inefficient to spend $300,000 (30 cents times a million sales) to save $200,000, the cost of the injury each year attributable to the feature that could be fixed for the $300,000. Some teachers, emphasizing that the law should strive for a level of deterrence that is economically optimal, might suggest that one should not impose tort liability in such a case because it would not be cost-justified to do so.
- Others might contend that imposing a strict form of liability—requiring the manufacturer to pay damages even though it was more expensive to prevent the accident than to have it happen—would itself lead to an efficient result if there were no "transaction costs."
- Many who would argue for manufacturer liability would do so on the grounds that morally, the law should not tolerate a crippling or disfiguring injury to even one child that could be avoided by a safety feature that would cost only 30 cents per unit. One might call this concept "moralizing compensa-

tion," contrasting it with the idea of "optimizing deterrence." One version of a morality-centered compensation approach would draw on social balance sheets with a broader view than that of efficiency accounting. In calculating social costs, for example, this approach might take into account the welfare burden on the community from injuries caused by technically efficient activities.

- Others might go further. They would make a moral judgment, apart from traditional conceptions of economic costs, that would in effect declare, "one crippling injury a year to a child is too many." They would insist on that position even though consumers as a whole might be willing, at least before the fact of injury, to take the risk of such injuries because they desire the product at the cheaper, pre-liability market price, even with its hazards. Our basic point is that the achievement of economically efficient results is not necessarily the whole story for law.

- Some people who focus on "corrective justice" would provide still a different rationalization of the problem of the toy injury. They might argue that the only crucial question is whether it is fair as between the manufacturer and the plaintiff to require the manufacturer to pay for the injury. They would suggest that this is the primary goal of justice, by contrast with efforts to influence the level of product hazards. They would add that individualized, corrective justice should even rule over moral judgments based on social considerations.

These different approaches illustrate that courts always must choose among competing rationales when they decide difficult cases. Among other things, they must consider the claim that there is only one rationale that governs a particular branch of the law as against the argument that an important task of courts is to decide which of several rationales is best applied in a particular case.

11

Remedies

The business end of the law lies in the remedies it offers. A court could tell a defendant in a tort suit that she was negligent, or could scold a defendant in a contract action for breaking a promise. Usually, however, that will not satisfy a plaintiff who has gone to the expense and anguish of a lawsuit. Except for the few plaintiffs who seek only vindication, those who are successful in litigation will always pose the practical question to the court, "What will you do about the defendant's behavior?" The remedy provides the answer.

Legal and Equitable Remedies

One way to divide the world of remedies is between legal remedies and equitable remedies. The principal legal remedy is damages—ordering one party to pay money to another, usually with the specific purpose of providing some sort of recompense to the claimant. A typical remedy in equity is to require the defendant to take some action or to prohibit the defendant from a course of conduct.

Damages

When a court orders a payment of money damages, the measure of damages becomes important. Some damage remedies seek to give back to the plaintiff what he has lost "out of pocket." Others aim to give the plaintiff the "benefit of her bargain"—for example, the value of what she was promised by a contract that was breached. Certain damage remedies try to compensate for intangible losses, for example, by attempting to assign money values to harms like pain and suffering. Some such categories of intangibles, although they are difficult to quantify on a neatly principled basis, are nonetheless well-established.

Punitive damages are a separate, and presently controversial, type of remedy that plaintiffs may seek. Courts assign a cluster of rationales to support the award of punitive damages. Unlike the more usual damage awards in both tort and contract cases, punitive damages are not designed for t..e purpose of compensation but rather, as the term suggests, to punish the defendant. Courts also rationalize punitive damages as a way to achieve an extra "sting" to deter defendants from very risky or highly culpable behavior, and even as a device for effectively reimbursing the plaintiff for her attorney's fees.

Equitable Remedies and Related Categories

Equity began as a system of courts that dispensed justice when common law courts could not provide an adequate remedy. It has now become a system of remedies administered by trial courts generally. Wearing their equity hats, courts possess a flexible battery of these remedies. They recognize that sometimes money cannot redress a wrong effectively, let alone prevent an injury, and that the best remedy may be one that compels or prohibits some kind of action. This section summarizes a few of the most-used equitable remedies.

Injunctions

A classic equitable remedy is the injunction, of which the most well-known is the prohibitory injunction—an order by the court that the defendant must cease or refrain from doing something. A typical example would be to stop the discharge of pollutants into the air or water.

Sometimes courts will order individuals to do something rather than to stop doing it. These mandatory orders, which may be called injunctions or which may have different labels, might command a party to do something like install pollution control equipment. A court may condition a *damages* remedy on a mandatory injunction: if the defendant obeys the mandatory order, it will not have to pay damages.

There are several sub-classes in the injunction category for which the time element is crucial. Sometimes even without prior notice to the defendant, a court may issue a *temporary restraining order* ("TRO"), which immediately prohibits the defendant from conduct in which it has been engaging, for example, dumping chemicals in a waterway or harassing a spouse. The court may do this in situations in which it is not ready to make a definitive ruling about the legality of the defendant's conduct, but in which the plaintiff will suffer "irreparable injury" if the court does not act right away to stop the defendant.

After the court holds a hearing, it may elect to go to the next stage, the *preliminary injunction,* which orders the defendant to continue to refrain from the conduct at issue. If the parties cannot work out a satisfactory settlement, the litigation will then proceed to a trial. At that stage, the court must make an unequivocal judgment about whether the defendant should be permitted to engage in that behavior. If it concludes, on reflection, that the behavior is illegal or unreasonable, it will enter a *permanent injunction.*

Specific Performance

Specific performance is a very special kind of equitable remedy involving an order to do something. Occasionally awarded in contracts cases, this remedy seeks to achieve a result that, in some sense, money could not buy. Suppose that A contracts to sell B a mountainside house with a spectacular view of hills and valleys. A backs out of the deal, but offers to pay damages to B that represent B's expenses in getting ready to move. He even offers to compensate B for the recent increase in price of a nearby house, lower on the mountain than A's house, that B could have bought earlier at a lower price. B counters that there is no other house that has a view like A's house. The court might order A to convey his house to B because of the uniqueness of the harm—the loss of ownership of a house that arguably could not be compensated in money.

One should note that it will take a lot to persuade a court to compel specific performance, a drastic remedy. Often, important policies will weigh against requiring a promisor to do what he has promised. For example, a court would be very reluctant to order someone to perform a surgical operation even though he or she was the best surgeon in the region for that type of procedure and had promised to do the operation. In support of a decision denying the specific performance remedy, the court might say that ordering people to perform personal services directly for others has an overtone of compelling slavery.

Constructive Trusts

One other example of an equitable remedy is the constructive trust. Suppose that C, the beneficiary of an insurance policy on D's life, murders D for the insurance money. E, who is D's only heir, brings an action against the insurance company for the proceeds on the policy, which otherwise would go to C under the terms of the policy. The court may impose a so-called "constructive trust" on the proceeds in favor of E. That is not what we ordinarily think of as a trust—a fund voluntarily set up by a moneyed person for named beneficiaries. Rather, a constructive trust is a remedy by which a court orders someone who has legal title to money or other property, but whose title has been acquired wrongfully or in violation of some equitable principle, to convey that property to a person who has an equitable right to it. In creating a "constructive trust," the court in effect stamps E's name on the insurance fund.

From a linguistic point of view, this is an example of something we mentioned above:[1] courts investing words that have well-accepted connotations with a meaning that rings rather oddly to ordinary persons. We can assure you, though, that after you come in contact with enough of these artificial usages, you will come to use them just like you employ ordinary language. We add one general hint. When a court uses the word "constructive" to modify another

---

[1] See pages 63-65.

word, it is likely that it is cloaking the other word with a special legal meaning.

The Distinction Between "Substance" and "Procedure"

It is useful, in discussing remedies, to mention a distinction that courts routinely make between "substantive" and "procedural" rules. For simplifying purposes, we might think of procedure as a series of gateways and roads, through and on which litigants travel through the courts. By contrast, substantive rules would be measuring rods to guide the actual resolution of disputes. One place where the difference is especially important is federal court litigation involving diversity of citizenship, because the federal court must apply state substantive law (for example, the law of contracts) but must conduct its proceedings according to the Federal Rules of Civil Procedure.

In practice, the distinction is not always easy. Consider, for example, the matter of statutes of limitations. Every state has legislation that sets time limits for the filing of lawsuits, usually attaching a specific time period to particular classes of litigation. For example, a contracts statute of limitations may impose a four-year limit on suits for breach of contract, measured from the time of the breach.

For various reasons, the question sometimes will arise whether a statute of limitations is procedural or substantive. Is it clear to you what the answer is? Some people would argue that because the statute performs essentially a gatekeeping function for the remedial power of courts, it is procedural. Others would say that because a statute of limitations keeps someone from enforcing a legal right, it is substantive. We do not propose to settle the argument, about which you will learn in your civil procedure class—only to alert you to the distinction between substantive and procedural rules, which will confront you in many legal contexts.

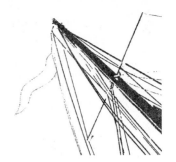

12

Legal Writing

Good "legal writing" ought to be like any good writing. When you read legal documents that contain jargon, that use language in a fuzzy way, or that are poorly organized, you are reading not just bad legal writing, but bad writing. Many lawyers write well, though, and everyone can improve his or her writing significantly.

The best writing habits grow over periods of years. If you have not been reading well-written prose for a long time, and you have not had teachers who forced you to rewrite and rewrite again, you start at a disadvantage. We do not kid ourselves, or you, that this little chapter will make you a good writer. Nor do we suggest that it represents a comprehensive introduction to legal writing, which your separate course in that subject will provide. What we hope it will do is identify some of the most common problems that occur in the writing of law students, and to suggest ways to solve those problems. Because we must begin by focusing on problems, a fair amount of the advice that follows is negatively phrased. When we can, however, we will try to say what to do rather than what not to do.

Should you have any doubt about how crucial writing is to attorneys, we suggest that you ask any lawyer you know whether writing is important to his or her work. We expect that the answer will line up with the result of a recent survey of young Chicago lawyers, who ranked oral and written communication as the "clear winners" among the important skills in legal practice.[1]

---

[1] Bryant G. Garth and Joanne Martin, Law Schools and the Construction of Competence, 43 J. Leg. Ed. 469, 474 (1993).

The text of this chapter focuses on principal problems of structure and organization. An appendix gives advice on how to avoid a few specific recurrent problems. In general, we advise that you pay careful attention to your legal writing course. The skills you learn in that course will be important to your summer jobs, and vital to the rest of your professional work.

Having a Purpose and Audience In Mind

Before you begin to write anything, you must have an idea of what you want to accomplish. Do you want to tell someone you love him or her? Convince your credit card issuer that you did not incur a particular charge? Order a winter jacket from a catalog? If you are a lawyer, or are studying law, questions about your purpose are more likely to run in this vein: Do you want to convince a court that your client has a better case than does an opponent? Are you trying to explain to a client how to avoid litigation? Do you want to persuade a professor that you have analyzed a hypothetical problem intelligently? If you are a judge, are you attempting to explain why a sympathetic plaintiff must lose because the law is against her? Keep the purpose of your writing, the identity of your reader, and your reader's needs and expectations firmly in mind. Composition teachers and rhetoricians call this writing for your audience.

One characteristic common to both your professional and lay readers is that they will be busy people. Thus, they will appreciate clarity and brevity in what they read. Indeed, not only will they appreciate those qualities, but your job may depend on them.

Organize Your Thoughts

Tied in closely with purpose is organization. A piece of paper before you is blank, neutral about your thoughts. You can put anything down on it you wish; the paper makes no judgments. It is you who must give content to the brief, or the memo, or the exam, and you who must organize the content to communicate effectively and to meet the expectations of your reader. A good writer organizes to provide information in the order in which her reader expects and needs that information.

Some people organize best by literally outlining their thoughts. When you outline your analysis of a legal issue, you break it down into its logical components. For example, when you analyze a claim that has a fixed definition, such as an intentional tort claim, you should organize the claim into its elements. Alternatively, if you analyze a claim for which the court must balance several factors, you might organize by discussing each of the factors and then comparing their importance.

If you analyze a battery claim—let us say a problem like the case in Chapter 2 in which someone yanked away a tray held by another—you might start with this familiar form:

I. Battery tort
   A. Intent
   B. Contact
   C. Harmful or Offensive
   D. Unprivileged
   E. Unconsented

On each element concerning which a legal issue exists, you would then proceed in this fashion: (1) Define the element (for example, what a contact requires in that jurisdiction). (2) Summarize the facts of the precedents relevant to that element (kicking a dog on a leash is contact with the person holding the leash). (3) Apply the law developed in the precedents to the facts of the case at issue (the dog on the leash is analogous to the tray in the hand). (4) Draw a conclusion about whether the facts fulfill that element (yanking the tray fulfills the contact element of a battery).

That is a time tested way to organize, by the elements of a claim, as well as a time tested way to analyze each element. Many students, however, do not start with an easy flow of ideas. They may need to kick-start themselves. These students may best begin to get a feel for the organization of a problem when they start writing prose sentences. The process of writing helps them to organize. If your mind works that way, you will find that as you write, your mind will start to move logically from one idea to another. In fact, even people who take naturally to the traditional outline form will find that the process of writing helps them to see relationships among parts of the material that they did not discern at first.

An important thing to keep in mind as you outline is that outlines are by their nature rough drafts, as is the prose version you first write from your outline. You should assume that your writing will change, for the better, as you get more of a grasp on the subject and as you rewrite your early drafts.

Logical Flow of Ideas; Transitions; The Problem of Jerky Sentences

An outline should make clear how the parts of your topic relate to each other. The best writing flows and carries the reader forward. If the information is not organized well, or a sentence is not clear, your reader has to go back and figure out what you mean. When you re-read a paragraph you have written—it may be a good test to read it aloud—you should ask yourself whether the ideas in the paragraph *connect* to one another.

A recurrent weakness in student writing is the series of jerky, unconnected sentences that require the reader to go back to connect up the information herself in order to understand its content. To provide a bad example, let us suppose King Henry V had said, addressing his army before a great battle against the French at Agincourt:

"We're all English. We should fight together like brothers today. I'm a king. You're like a brother to me if you fight with me."

***

Now compare what Shakespeare had the king say:

"We few, we happy few, we band of brothers;
For he to-day that sheds his blood with me

Shall be my brother; be he ne'er so vile,
Today shall gentle his condition."

We are not suggesting that you should wax poetic in a legal memorandum or brief. Indeed, you will want to fashion complete sentences, so we would advise against a construction like "We few, we happy few, we band of brothers." However, consider what Shakespeare does that you *can* imitate: He employs the word "for" to effect a transition. Even the words beginning "be he ne'er so vile" carry the reader forward.

Now notice how much better your draft in modern English prose would be, as contrasted with our original jerky example, if you added just a couple of words at strategic places to tie your ideas together: "We are like brothers today; for if you fight with me, it is as if you were my brother. Although I am a king and you are a peasant, fighting alongside me here will make you noble."

In emphasizing the need to link up your ideas, we understand that the logical linkage between those ideas may seem absolutely clear to you when you construct jerky sentences. When you write, "I'm a king. You're a brother to me if you fight with me," it may be apparent to you, in your own mind, that what you are saying is, "I am a king and you are a peasant, but if you fight with me today, you will be like my brother." But you are not saying that; you are leaving the reader to supply the linkage between your two sentences. Notice what even the little word "but" does in our later version; it provides a transition and a logical link. Since reading is hard work as it is, your aim should be to make the job as smooth for the reader as possible. It is the fulfillment of that task that makes good writing itself hard work.

Active Voice

Consider the following sentence, which uses the passive voice:
"Sentences were written by Jim with subjects before verbs."
Now consider whether this version would make the point more sharply:
"Jim wrote his sentences using active voice."

Would you award the prize to the first sentence or the second one? It should be clear that "Jim wrote his sentences" is superior to "Sentences were written by Jim." The second sentence is also shorter.

When you read these examples, you may think that the "sentences were written" sentence is a caricature, a joke. As teachers, however, we see hundreds of passive sentences like that every year. Our aim is to give those sentences power by making them active, or, in trendy lingo, to empower the verbs.

Everyone yields to passive voice on occasion, often as a result of fatigue. Sometimes the problem is physical fatigue. Sometimes it is intellectual fatigue. In either case, you must fight through your tiredness against the passive voice. Until you develop the rhythm of positive expression, you might do well to do a separate passive-voice check on yourself every couple of pages that you write. We do not say that passive voice may not be superior to active voice on some occasions. For example, the use of passive voice may be desirable when you do not know who did an action, or when you want to de-emphasize who did an action. However, we assure you that most people do not have to worry about using the passive voice too seldom.

Besides checking your own drafts for passive voice, you may drill yourself on the writing of others—even other lawyers. To start close to home, you might scrutinize some pages at random in any of your casebooks, looking for the hated passive voice in judicial opinions. Think of ways that you might change an offending passive sentence to give it more punch. Illustrative of how simple the exercise can be are some variations on a sentence from a state court decision:

1) [Passive-passive: The worst] "It was held by another court that when a landlord represented that a bed was safe, an express warranty action could be maintained."

2) [Passive-active: Surely better] "It was held by another court that when a landlord represented that a bed was safe, the plaintiff could maintain an action based on the express warranty."

3) [Active-active: Is this the best?] "Another court held that when a landlord represented that a bed was safe, the plaintiff could sue for breach of express warranty."

This exercise incorporates some lessons that go beyond our campaign for active voice. We did several things in the third version to give it more force than even the second version. We made the first verb ("held") active. Having made the last verb active in the second version ("maintain"), we changed that verb to the shorter and generally more powerful "sue." We got rid of the phrase "based on," which adds very little, if anything, to the message we are trying to communicate.

We might further have changed the end of the sentence to read, "could sue on express warranty." This is a judgment call. Although "could sue on express warranty" saves words, the word "breach" conveys some connotations of wrongdoing that might impart thrust to the sentence. Moreover, the phrase "breach of express warranty" is somewhat more exact, and rather more graceful, than the phrase "on express warranty."

However you resolve such matters of taste and judgment, it is important to understand not only that active voice writing is powerful but that a preference for it is often not just a matter of taste but of choosing the better technique.

Consider how our anonymous writer of bad sentences might have constructed a speech of Brutus, proposing the murder of Caesar:

"He should be carved by us as a dish fit for the gods,
and not hacked up by us as a carcass fit for the hounds."

***

We hope you think Shakespeare did better:

"Let's carve him as a dish fit for the gods,
Not hew him as a carcass fit for hounds."

The first version is a bad example. The second version is a good example. That is not a judgment call.

Short Words, Short Sentences

The last quotation leads us to stress the value of simplicity and brevity. Notice that in Brutus's two lines of nineteen words (counting articles) above, there is just one word that is more than one syllable. And that word, "carcass," carries particular force in a sentence that proposes the assassination of an emperor.

The law has a l t of long words. There is no way that one can jam "tortfeasor" or "mortgagee" into one syllable. That, however, makes it even more important to the power of your writing that you keep the other words short and simple. Thus, if your first thought is to write, "The social problem addressed by this legislation is considerable and complicated," you might consider, "This statute aims to combat a great and complex evil in society." The latter sentence is active, and uses shorter and more emphatic nouns and verbs.

Here is another illustration. If your first draft says, "The subject of this litigation, involving a philosophically challenging problem in personal injury jurisprudence, is whether. . . ." we hope your next draft will start, "This case presents a difficult issue of tort law." You may think we exaggerate, but we see too many of the first type of sentences in these pairings and not enough of the second type. Judges would generally prefer to read the second type of sentence, which is lean and free of overblown language, in which an active verb immediately follows the subject, and in which the subject is a concrete rather than an abstract noun. The reason they would prefer it is the same reason you will prefer it, if you think about the matter; the second type communicates more effectively.

Brevity is often a virtue, so use one word when it will do a job that might otherwise consume several words. To illustrate, use

"Jones sued Smith"

instead of

"Jones brought an action against Smith."

Another good general rule, which parallels our suggestion that you use simple words and as few words as possible, is to keep your sentences short. We will give a bad example followed by a good example. For the bad example, consider the indented sentence just below, which tries to make the point we are now telling you about.

The sentence you are reading at this moment presents an idea that makes the lesson of brevity evident in another way that ties in with what we have said about simplicity of language and the use of relatively few words when you might be tempted to use a relatively great number of words, an idea that can be summarized by saying that you should attempt to write short sentences.

***

Now consider these two sentences:

The sentence you have just read gives an exaggerated example of our other major point about simplicity and brevity. That point is, keep your sentences short.

***

Notice that the two indented sentences just above present in 26 words, broken into two sentences, the same thought with which an eye-straining 67-word sentence consumed the first indented paragraph. Notice also, that when you break very long sentences into shorter ones, you can promote the flow between the sentences by carrying over an idea or word from the first sentence (in this case, the word "point"), to begin the second sentence.

We would suggest that practically all of the time, it will benefit you in your professional writing to work at achieving this style. Aim for shorter sentences, but mix your style so that your work does not read like, "Look, Jane, look. See Dick run."

We will close this Part with an excellent example of writing by a lawyer in a legal context, from a master of the craft. It is the paragraph in which Judge Cardozo presented his statement of the facts in *Palsgraf v. Long Island Railroad*, a case that appears in practically every Torts casebook:

> Plaintiff was standing on a platform of defendant's railroad after buying a ticket to go to Rockaway Beach. A train stopped at the station, bound for another place. Two men ran forward to catch it. One of the men reached the platform of the car without mishap, though the train was already moving. The other man, carrying a package, jumped aboard the car, but seemed unsteady as if about to fall. A guard on the car, who had held the door open, reached forward to help him in, and another guard on the platform pushed him from behind. In this act, the package was dislodged, and fell upon the rails. It was a package of small size, about fifteen inches long, and was covered by a newspaper. In fact it contained fireworks, but there was nothing in its appearance to give notice of its contents. The fireworks when they fell exploded. The shock of the explosion threw down some scales at the other end of the platform many feet away. The scales struck the plaintiff, causing injuries for which she sues.[2]

Taken together, these sentences have something in common, something that you can emulate, even if you cannot capture Cardozo's special grace. The sentences are varied, with only two sentences being in the passive voice.[3] The subjects and the verbs come close together. The sentences move the reader forward from one event or thought to another. They are short: in a long paragraph, only one is more than 20 words, and that one only 27. These sentences *march*, and they are clear.

---

[2] Palsgraf v. Long Island R.R. Co., 162 N.E. 99 (N.Y. 1928).

[3] Perhaps Justice Cardozo wrote one of those sentences using the words, "the package was dislodged," in the passive instead of active voice because he did not want to focus on the guard's role. Justice Cardozo concluded that the railroad was not liable for Ms. Palsgraf's injuries.

Citation Form

Your course on legal research will introduce you to citation form, probably accompanying this training with the small volume popularly called the "Bluebook."[4] This reference will give you scores of rules about how to "cite" sources. There is usually some logic to those principles, but whether you discern the logic or not, you must follow the rules, if for no other reason than uniformity.

Think of all the ways that you might cite the great 1916 case of *MacPherson v. Buick Motor Company*, which appears at page 382 of volume 217 of the New York Reports, and also at page 1050 of Volume 111 of the Northeast Reporter. The pre-1991 uniform citation style for this case, requiring what are known are parallel citations, was MacPherson v. Buick Motor Co., 217 N.Y. 382, 111 N.E. 1050 (1916). You will find that style in law reviews and many cases published before 1991 (not all cases, because many courts use their own citation forms.) The post-1991 Bluebook requires the following simpler citation, which omits the reference to the New York Reports and uses only the reference to the Northeast ("regional") reporter: MacPherson v. Buick Motor Co., 111 N.E. 1050 (N.Y. 1916). One could invent other citation rules. For example, one could require the use of MacPherson's first name, or the spelling out of "Company," or the spelling out of "New York" and "Northeast." The overriding value, whatever the rule, is that of uniformity. Unvarying rules relieve writers and editors of decisions that would otherwise be unnecessarily time-consuming, besides achieving the principal goal of allowing readers to find the source of the citation easily.

It is possible to engage in philosophical arguments about citation style, and sometimes you may disagree with a particular uniform citation. However, no matter how frustrating the task, you must learn the style adopted at your school and slavishly follow it. As a practical matter, as a first-year student you will be using a few citation forms over and over again, and will have to look up others as they become relevant. The sooner you get into your head the most-used forms, the easier you will feel about not having to wrestle constantly with the mechanics of supporting your arguments. But, at the beginning, it

---

[4] Some law schools use a somewhat different version of citation in the "Maroon Book."

will take you a long time to learn to cite cases and statutes in your written work. For your first assignments, you may spend several hours on citation form and you may hate every minute of it. As you practice more, you will be able to write the more common citations as a matter of course.

Practice, Practice, Practice

We have the pleasure every year of seeing some very good student writing. Yet however well students write, like anyone else they can always improve their writing. The key, for those who write well or less well, is to practice good writing. You will no more learn to write better without practice than you will improve at playing the piano or playing shortstop without practice. It is also crucial to start work on your written assignments very early.

There is no royal road to writing well, but one quick fix is to spare a moment now and then to focus critically on a specific piece of writing. It may be useful to select a few passages in something you have to read for class, although any written material will do. Fix on a sentence, or a paragraph, that does not seem to communicate very well. Try analyzing it to see where it is weak. Rewrite it. Then rewrite your rewrite. This process will help to emphasize what a responsibility it is to write, but it also will underline the opportunity that writing presents to you.

Naturally, we advise the same fierce attention to rewriting of your own work. Start your assignments early enough to allow you time to rewrite. It is always possible, we concede, that you might have gotten something right on the first try. But almost always, you can improve a piece of writing by rewriting it. Hemingway rewrote the ending of *A Farewell to Arms* thirty-five times.

When you do rewrite, keep in mind some basic principles we presented above. Remember who your audience is, and your purpose in writing. Write clearly, simply, and with active sentences. Keep your sentences reasonably short, and tie them together logically.

We will add an irritating postscript: Make sure you spell correctly. You may have to deal with a judge, or a partner, or even a professor, who learned to spell before Spell-Check, which means that he or she *really* learned to spell. That person will know the difference between "principal" and "principle." Spell-Check does not.

Appendix: Common Problems in Writing That Can Be Fixed

This Appendix presents solutions to a few problems that frequently afflict student writing.

SUBJECT-VERB AGREEMENT

Plural subjects have plural verbs and singular subjects have singular verbs:

- "These statistics indicate," rather than "These statistics indicates."
- "This class of victims is not typical," rather than "This class of victims are not typical." Observe that the subject of the verb "is" is "class," not "victims."

Students often make errors in subject-verb agreement because they insert so many words and phrases between the subject and the verb that they lose track of which word is the subject. Correct this problem, and write sentences that are easier to understand, by keeping the subject and verb as close together as possible.

REFERENTS

Specify referents for words that are otherwise indefinite. Consider this passage:

The court had established that the interest in emotional security deserves the same protection as the interest in physical integrity. In the *Smith* case, the court had hoped to take it one step further.

The writer of this sentence would have made her meaning clearer by saying, in the second sentence, ". . . the court had hoped to take this principle one step further." Some people might argue that this is a judgment call, but we use this example to stress that when you are using a word for which you have not clearly established a referent, you should err on the side of clarifying that referent. The edited clause does this by substituting "this principle" for the indefinite word "it." Some writers might spell out the referent even more specifically: ". . . the court had hoped to take the principle of protection for mental interests one step further." At some point, it is true, the addition of extra words will get verbose and awkward. The last example may be at that point. Always consider, however, how much more awkward it is when your meaning is not clear.

THE DANGLING MODIFIER

Most people probably do not consider dangling modifiers to be sinful, at least if sin is measured by what people write without thinking they have erred. However, the dangling modifier is still wrong, whether it is a sin or not. When you see the participle form in a word that ends in "ing" at the beginning of one of your sentences, be especially critical of yourself.

Let us say that you want to communicate that after a body of precedent had limited tort recovery to physical injury, a court allowed recovery for emotional harm. Now consider this description: "Flowing from the principle of protecting interests in bodily integrity, the court protected emotional interests." What is wrong with this sentence, given the meaning you wish to impart, is that it was not the court that "flowed"; it was the development of the law as it moved beyond the protection of one interest to protect another. It would be better to write, "Moving beyond the principle of protecting interests in bodily integrity, the court began to protect emotional interests." Here, it *is* the court that "moves," so your "moving" participle does not dangle, and the subject and the participle agree. Alternatively, if you insist on keeping the image of a "flow" in the sentence, you could write, "Flowing from the principle of protecting physical interests was the idea that courts should also protect emotional interests." Here, it *is* the "idea" that is "flowing."

If you believe we are being picky here, consider a more obvious example:

"Having been dead for 24 hours, the searchers found the victim's body." Even if you think that dangling modifiers are not sins, you can see that it was not the searchers who had been dead for 24 hours. Thus, we reiterate that when you find yourself starting sentences with "ing" verb forms—which, we emphasize, can be perfectly good vehicles of communication—be on guard against error.

APOSTROPHES

Apostrophes primarily serve two purposes: to form possessives and to form contractions. Many people use apostrophes where they are not needed; it is hard for many people to avoid wrong uses because one sees them used incorrectly so often.

1. Possessives:

a. You make a noun possessive by adding 's. The apostrophe distinguishes a singular possessive noun from a plural noun. To form the plural of most nouns, you add just an s, not an apostrophe.

- Plural: The plaintiffs argue. "Plaintiffs" is a plural noun. More than one plaintiff did the arguing.
- Possessive: The plaintiff's argument was brief. "Plaintiff's" is singular possessive. The argument involved is that of one plaintiff.

b. To form the possessive of a singular word that ends in s, you almost always add 's. There are a few exceptions, which you can find in a style or usage book.

- Jones's argument was long. "Jones's" is the possessive of one Ms. Jones.

c. However, you form the plural possessive by adding an apostrophe to a plural noun that already ends in s. To form the possessive of a plural noun that does not end in s, add 's.

- The plaintiffs' argument was long. "Plaintiffs'" is plural possessive. The argument involved is that of more than one plaintiff.

- The children's playroom was being painted. "Children's" is plural possessive. The playroom is for the use of more than one child.

d. You use an apostrophe to show a plural in one situation: the plural of numbers and letters in order to avoid confusion.

- This word is spelled with three e's.

e. Do not use an apostrophe for possessive pronouns. The most confusing possessive pronoun for most people is "its." "Its" means that something belongs to it. There is no apostrophe.

- The court convened late. Its time schedule was completely awry. "Its" here is possessive, referring to the court's schedule. If you had spelled the word as "it's," you would have written the contraction for "it is."

2. *Contractions:*

Use an apostrophe for a contraction where a letter is omitted.

- It's always wrong not to inform your client of progress in the case. Here, "it's" is a contraction of the words "it is." Unlike the possessive "its," the "it's" requires an apostrophe.
- "There's nothing new to report." "There's" is a contraction of the words "there is."

Contractions are a fairly informal way of speaking. You should not use them in memoranda and especially not in writing to a court.

13

Studying and Reviewing

Most law students find that law school, at least the first year, requires the hardest studying they have ever had to do. That is not surprising. Law school requires you, all at once, to absorb a different method of approaching problems, to learn a new language, to use new sources of information, and to employ a different technique of taking examinations.

This chapter offers a few basic suggestions about how to make your studying effective. As you seek to develop study habits that are productive for law school, you should take comfort in the fact that hundreds of thousands of people have done that with reasonable success.

How To Study, Generally

One of the most important requirements for effective law study, which is good preparation for law practice, is to manage your time. Especially during certain weeks of law school, you will feel that there simply is not enough time to do what needs to be done. And you will be right. As we have remarked before, you will find that everything takes longer than you think it will. That is because everything is new to you, and that is why it is crucial to organize and to set priorities.

A useful principle is to establish guidelines for how you use your time. Set target amounts of time to study, or to do the required research and writing, for each course. One should not be rigid about this sort of planning. That is why we say "guidelines." It may turn out that contracts, which usually takes two and a half hours to prepare per class, will require three tonight, because the assignment is longer or more complex than usual. Or it may happen that because the assignment is benignly manageable, you will require only two hours.

The decision that recurs is where you should put that extra half hour. That is the priorities issue. It comes up in diverse ways, some of which involve choices that may total quite a number of hours to be allocated in one way or another over the course of a semester. Should you work harder on the course you think you understand best, hoping for an A or even an A plus rather than a B plus, and slack off on the course that you like least, assuming that in that course you can't do better than B but won't do worse than C plus? Should you reread your memorandum assignment one more time before it is due? We cannot answer questions like that for you. We do suggest you study subjects that seem hardest to you when you are freshest and least subject to frustration. Again, particular choices day by day are matters for your judgment. We also note the possibility that the course you like least may be the course in which you do best on the exam or the written assignment. Grades can be difficult to predict, and we recommend that you do not give up on any of your courses.

If you feel at sea the first few weeks of law school, struggling to manage your time, you should understand that everyone else is in the same boat. Moreover, you will be pleased to know that things will almost certainly get better. But not right away. Experience helps you to set priorities. We can also assure you that the experience of setting priorities in law school will prepare you for an even more difficult challenge—doing it in practice.

The Study Group Question

You will have to decide for yourself, perhaps after some experimentation, whether you want to join a study group, and how much you want to participate in jointly producing outlines. The way you study best—which may take some experimentation to find out as you confront this new discipline—will dictate this entirely personal choice.

A main consideration is time, and here you may wish to play economist. Does the benefit you get from the time spent in discussions with your group exceed the benefit you would receive from studying by yourself? Of course, you could crank into your equation the social features of the group. If you do join a group, it will develop its own culture and its own rules about who contributes what—which may include congeniality, brownies, or a special feel for the Federal Rules of Civil Procedure. You may have to figure in disadvantages as well as benefits. One member of your group may be personally obnoxious as well as brilliant. Whatever the factors that develop as the relevant ones, you must clarify your own priorities in making the basic decision about whether to join, or stay in, a study group.

When groups form, other people sometimes may feel they are being left out of cliques. Keeping that in mind, you should understand that either joining or not joining is an entirely normal choice. After surveying the scene, you should do what is best for you. In any event, remember that you can learn a lot from talking about your law school subjects. If you decide not to join a study group, then try to explain topics to someone else, or even talk the subject to yourself when you are taking a walk or a shower.

Reviewing

Some time in each semester you should begin to review the material that is being covered in your courses. A lot of people do this by organizing course material into outline form; indeed, many students simply refer to reviewing as "outlining."

There is no mystery about why you must do this, apart from the idealistic motive of learning the law for its own sake because it is intellectually challenging, stimulating and intuitively interesting. The pragmatic reason one puts together course reviews is to prepare for examinations.

Many law professors are now experimenting with ways, other than final exams, to assess students' abilities and their mastery of subject matter. This discussion, however, tends to focus on preparation for "traditional" law school examinations, the kind that most students will continue to face in many subjects. As you get a feel for the requirements of particular courses, in some cases you will want to modify the techniques that we suggest here.

Law school examinations typically feature hypothetical problems, often invented by the professor, that seek to test the student's developed ability to analyze the material presented in a particular course. Your task in reviewing is to prepare yourself to deal with those problems, or indeed any questions designed to test your command of the subject.

The Outline

The function of a review sheet, or outline, is to establish a framework of analysis for legal problems. Your goal is to deal with two interlinked bodies of knowledge and ability that professors will try to test: (1) Your knowledge of "rules" at a level from which you can apply those rules logically to particular problems (2) Your ability to apply the rules you have learned to new sets of facts, and to resolve the ambiguities and analyze the probable outcomes of such problems.

You should organize your outline by topics, not by cases. A good way to choose your topics headings is to use the titles of the casebook chapters and their sections and subsections. The information you include under each topic will come primarily from the cases and statutes in each section, but will also include material from the notes and comments in your casebook and from class discussions.

The course in civil procedure provides a good illustration. Almost certainly, a significant part of an examination in that course will test your understanding of the principal procedural checkpoints in litigation, which may be dealt with in separate chapters in your book. Thus, for example, your outline will include the highlights of what you have learned about the motion to dismiss. It should refer to the Federal Rule of Civil Procedure, Rule 12(b)(6), which provides for that motion. It should include short summaries (sometimes in just a few words, if you can boil them down that far) of cases that help to define the issues involved in the question of when a court should, and should not, grant a motion to dismiss. If there are cases in the coursebook that present differing points of view on the same question—that is, two opposed decisions or majority and dissenting opinions in the same case—it would be useful to summarize the disagreement between opposing judges. A principal reason for this is that, often, controversial questions present an excellent opportunity for a professor to write an exam problem. Exactly because they are controversial, they help the professor to give you an opportunity to show your understanding of the difficulties of a problem, to weigh competing views, and to present a persuasive answer.

Besides summarizing cases, statutory provisions, and rules like the Rules of Civil Procedure, you should include in an outline anything that you think might be helpful in preparing you to show your relevant knowledge and your ability to resolve legal controversies. Perhaps the most obvious sources of outline material are questions that your professor asked in class and questions posed (or answers given) in the coursebook. It is only common sense that you should be careful to take notes on the professor's questions in class, since it is the professor who makes up and grades the exam. In fact, some of your most important notes may be those questions. They sometimes will reveal what the professor thinks are the most interesting issues in the course, which have a way of winding up on exams.

Your professor or your coursebook may discuss competing interpretations of the law and the policy bases of specific legal rules; you will want to note such discussions. It also would be prudent to note particular ideas or phrases—even "buzz words"—that seem especially important or that appear to appeal to your professor. As one student said to one of us recently, "You have to walk the walk and talk the talk." That's your professor's walk and talk. He or she will grade your examination.

Your outline also might include ideas you have gleaned from treatises and hornbooks, as well as from law review articles that your coursebook cites, that your professor mentions, or that you have found yourself. Many students find useful explanations in commercially published outlines.   However, we strongly caution against sole, or even principal, reliance on such outlines. The reason, which we amplify below, is that the value of an outline comes from making it yourself.

At least the ideal of an outline is that it will be your own little treatise or hornbook on the subject of a course. The reason you fashion this little treatise is to prepare you, under the conditions of an examination, to analyze an unfamiliar problem case and discuss it in light of the principles and concepts that you have learned in the course.

Many people do their reviewing literally in outline form because an outline enables them to place course material in an orderly framework and to see how different topics of the course relate to one another. The function of an outline is, after all, to help you to organize the material so that you will be able to see the issues in examination problems and discuss those issues with both knowledge and under- standing. (Chapter 14 treats techniques for writing exams.)

Illustrations of Outlines

Here are two examples of outlines, offered purely for illustration of format. One uses material that is likely to be familiar in first year curriculums, the subject of torts. The other example is from Estates and Trusts, a course that is typically an upper-year course. Both examples illustrate, in an abbreviated way, a form that identifies particular elements of the course, using specific applications and giving information about where the maker of the outline found the material.

1. Battery

Here is an example of an outline of the tort of battery. The material in parentheses provides examples of the source of the point discussed.

I. BATTERY
    A. Contact — results in a physical touching of the person; can be indirect touching—the defendant need not directly touch the plaintiff.

1. Examples
—Plaintiff hits the ground after the defendant pulls a chair from under her (*Garratt v. Dailey*, casebook p. 33).
—Defendant yanks a plate from the plaintiff's hand; this might be deemed a battery because the object is so closely connected with the plaintiff (class discussion).
2. Rationale for not requiring direct touching: Battery emphasizes dignitary interest, and yanking the plate violates that interest.

B. Intent
1. Meaning
Purpose (ordinary meaning of intent for lawyers as well as non-lawyers).
Knowledge with substantial certainty that there will be a harmful or offensive contact (*Garratt v. Dailey*, p. 33, five-year-old defendant).
2. Rationale for lesser standard of knowledge with substantial certainty:
—Differentiates intentional torts from negligence, which requires foreseeability of harmful consequences, whereas this standard requires only knowledge of at least offensive contact.
—Demands compensation from persons, even those who cannot foresee actual harm, "who violate social norms and injure innocent people."
—Standard even applies to children.

C. Intended contact must be harmful or offensive
1. Examples
Harmful—Actual physical injury *(Kelly v. Grimsky*, p. 42).
Offensive—In a manner that breaches social norms concerning personal dignity; a less demanding test for the plaintiff than "harmful": Kicking a schoolmate in the shin, even without intending actual harm, when class has been called to order (*Vosburg v. Putney*, p. 27)
2. Explanation and rationale for lesser requirement of "offensive":

—Violation of a social norm—the decorum of the classroom—justifies the imposition of tort damages even if the person who did the act did not intend actual physical injury;

—Discourages people from disobeying society's rules; moreover, as between a completely innocent person and someone who violated a rule even though he did not intend injury, it is fair that the rule violator should have to pay for the loss.

***

2. Wills

Part of an outline for a wills course could be:

I. REQUIREMENTS OF EXECUTING A WILL
    A. Signature: every jurisdiction requires
        1. Purposes of requirement: Gulliver article
        —Shows that testator adopted the writing as final; not a preliminary draft
        —Provides evidence of whose will
        —Prevents fraudulent wills
        2. Jurisdictions that don't require signature at "foot or end":
           a. *Estate of Wineburg* (casebook p. 86): testator wrote her name only in the opening paragraph of the will: "This is Opal Wineburg's will." Intended only as an identification, not as signature adopting the will as hers.
           b. But, opening handwritten paragraph with the words, "This is my will, Joy Smith," shows signature intended to adopt the will. *Estate of Smith* (p. 97).
           c. Problem of how can "adopt" a document that not written yet.
        3. Jurisdictions that require at foot or end.

The Strategy of Reviewing

In an ideal world, you would start reviewing each course at about the sixth week of a semester, give or take a week, and you would squeeze out enough time to review each course each succeeding weekend. In the real world, most people will not do that. On a given Sunday afternoon when they "ought" to be reviewing, they may want to take a walk, or visit parents or friends, or watch television. Or they may have a legal memorandum due on Monday.

With all of that reality check in mind, remember that the more you rework an outline, the more you will understand. This is because as you keep going over a body of material, you learn it more meaningfully. Your outline in the eleventh week of a semester will exhibit more understanding of material to which you originally were exposed in the sixth week than you derived when you initially reviewed in the seventh week, because the later review provides a broader framework.

The operational lesson is that reviewing a law course is a lot like piano practice, or studying calculus, or learning how to cook. The more you do, on average, the more you will get out of the enterprise. It is true that some students say that they have done better on certain exams for which they studied lightly than exams for which they prepared diligently. But averages are important, and in general, the keys are commitment and effort.

A serious strategic question eventually arises late in any semester: How much more *new* work should you do on your outline? We do not have a pat answer for that question. We can say only that at some point, you will decide that you have no more time to learn more details about the intricacies of motions for directed verdict, or what it takes to create an offer in contracts, or the elements of adverse possession in property.

It is at that point that your thirst for learning must turn pragmatically to a thirst for internalizing. Many students will tell you that in the real world, this means "memorizing." We use the seemingly more idealistic word "internalizing" because if you do enough reviewing of material that you have prepared, or played a meaningful part in preparing, then you will begin to absorb the material. It will become part of you in a way that just memorizing-to-disgorge does not achieve. To nail down the point, the fact that you prepared the material will make it more meaningful, and thus more instructive, than trying to memorize a commercial outline done by someone else who has not taken your particular class with your particular teacher.

We conclude on a note that may sound sermonizing, but we believe it describes how to get the most out of courses, usually in terms of your actual knowledge and frequently even on the grade sheet. Whether the issue is how much work you do in any one semester, or in any one course, or for any one class period, the crucial personal choice is how much you want to put into the enterprise.

14

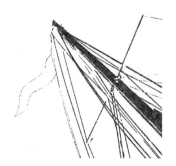

Exams

Examinations are not particularly pleasant occasions for anyone, including professors. Remember, we have to grade them. The good news is that exams can be learning experiences, especially if one views the whole examination process broadly to include the activity of preparing for exams. Indeed, the principal part of the learning occurs in the process of reviewing, described in the last chapter. If you put some time into that task, we guarantee that you will find a course more interesting than if you do not; you will see relationships in the materials that a more casual eye would not have discerned.

Solid preparation for an exam also increases the chance that the activity of writing the exam will itself be rewarding. After all, an examination should give you an opportunity to show what you know and, within certain limits, to be creative with that knowledge.

Stop babbling and get down to it, you say. How do you write a law school examination?

Some Preliminary Disclaimers

This chapter identifies what we perceive as major opportunities in exam-taking and problems that students can remedy, at least to some extent. However, as careful lawyers, we want to limit our warranty with a couple of observations.

First, what we say here applies most focally to "traditional" law school essay examinations. We are talking most specifically about exams that consist principally of hypothetical problems fashioned to test your knowledge of a particular course and your ability to use that knowledge in an analytical fashion by applying the law you have studied to the hypothetical facts. We will not specifically discuss the type of exam question that asks you to evaluate particular goals or policies of the law while not necessarily placing the question in a factual context.

We believe that the advice in this chapter will be useful to those questions and to your other law school work as well, and indeed generally to your future work as a lawyer. However, our focus is on the traditional law exam format, which typically will require you to write an analysis of a few questions drawn from the topics covered during the semester.

Second, we must note that at some point, talent will make a difference. When a runner wants to know how to improve his or her place in races, there are various tips that can help—about the start, the stride, and even how to lean into the tape. There comes a time, however, when the coach can say only, "Run faster." We cannot tell you how to attain the level of aptitude that the class genius possesses—how to "run faster." We do believe, however, that what we advise below will help you gain an extra stride here and there.

Key Word Outlines; Open Book Exams

Many students find it useful, just before taking an exam, to prepare from their larger outline an outline consisting of key words that capture what they perceive to be the most important subject headings or concepts in the course. If an exam will be open book, students probably will carry in with them a sheet with this super-skeleton outline. If the exam is to be closed book, they memorize the skeleton outline fully. They may remember it well enough without writing it down. If not, when it is announced that the examination has begun, they will scribble down the memorized list on the first page or inside cover of the exam booklet for ready reference.

There is a difference of opinion about this kind of checklist. Some people think it helps you only marginally if at all. This is because whatever level of preparation you bring to the examination, the exam itself should inspire your recognition of each issue that a key word outline is designed to help you recognize. However, many students swear by such outlines, and in any event preparing one may provide a good last-minute review. Moreover, a key word outline may occasionally trigger a useful idea and help you remember some concepts that are relevant to exam problems. Our view is, any crutch in a storm, including psychological crutches.

We have to stress that if you are not ready when you walk into an exam, no open book or open outline is likely to help you very much. Some students think that if they are taking an open book exam they will be able after the exam starts to look through their casebook and their outlines to write their answers. We believe this is a mistake—you should go to every exam as if it were closed book. You will not have enough time to consult your materials except to refresh your memory about a few particular points.

Time Limits

Examinations have time limits. As one of our own teachers was fond of saying, the issue is not, "What are the best answers you can write on this exam?" Rather, it is, "What are the best answers you can write in three hours?" That probably is the average time for law school exams. Some teachers may give 24-hour take-home exams, but you may not regard that as a favor after you have endured one of those.

The main point is that you must gauge your time, whatever the limit is. Many professors will provide suggested time limits per question. Since they probably will roughly apportion their grading of different problems based on those suggestions, you would do well to follow them—not obsessively, but rather closely. The existence of time limits, as we shall emphasize in a moment, makes especially important for exams some advice we gave earlier about writing generally: organize and establish priorities.

Read The Question

It is vital that you read each question carefully. A serious mis-reading of a question is likely to produce proportionally adverse results. If you answer a question that a problem does not present, the professor has little to grade you on.

Many people read the whole exam first, or at least scan it, in order to familiarize themselves with it and get a sense of its overall scope. Even if you plunge right into the first question, read the whole question first to get an idea of the issues. If what you thought was the issue in Part A is certainly the issue in Part B, do some more thinking. Usually different parts of a problem will not focus on the same issue. You may have misread Part A but would not know it if you had not read the whole question first.

After a summary reading of each question, read the question again slowly with an eye to picking out the relevant details, that is, the details that are important to the issues you have identified. Zero in on the facts; most of them will be crucial to your answer. If your teacher has specified issues for you to discuss, stick to them. If she has not, then you must identify the issues.

Law school exams differ from certain kinds of undergraduate exams, on which you may have received credit for disgorging memorized material, or material that you happened to know but that was not particularly relevant. Successful law examination answers, like any successful legal work, stick to what is relevant to the issues the question raises. They use the facts in the problem that are crucial to the answer and they *apply* knowledge to the problems presented, analyzing those problems rather than just identifying them.

Organize Your Answer

It is important to organize your answer. How should one begin organizing? People vary in what works for them concerning initial organization of their writing. Some like to prepare a little outline for an answer before they begin actually writing it, perhaps scribbling the outline right on the question sheet. Some prepare elaborate outlines, although we do not recommend this approach because it takes so much time. Others will "write their way into the exam," pushing themselves to get some sentences on paper that respond to an issue. The process of writing itself helps them to organize as they proceed, especially as the adrenalin begins to flow. Then as they begin to think ahead, they may write a simple outline in the margin to help them remember what to include.

Our principal point is that you should do what works for you. However, the reader of an exam will appreciate it if she discerns a logical framework for your answer. That does not mean that the professor will not dig out the analysis if it is there. It does mean that between two answers that arrive at the same analytical conclusion, the one that shows its process of reasoning more clearly will receive the better grade. If that somehow seems unjust to you, ask yourself a couple of questions. Don't you think judges would value a logical progression of argument in briefs? Don't you think that clients would value organization in their lawyers' memoranda?

Yet sometimes getting started may be more important than meticulous organization. Because exams have time limits, it is vital to get yourself moving. As we have noted, starting to write usually helps to get the adrenalin going. Occasionally, if the first question leaves you cold, you may want to start with another question. Or if Part A of a question is temporarily a mystery, and you understand the issue in Part B, start with Part B. If you do that, be sure to label carefully the question, or part, that you are answering so that the teacher will follow what you have done.

When you discuss specific causes of action, whether common law claims or statutory ones, remember to organize these claims by the elements or factors of their definitions, and by the types of facts that the courts use to analyze each element or factor. For example, if your problem involves an intentional tort, you would set out each element of that tort. You would then focus your answer on the elements at issue. If one or more elements are not at issue, explain briefly why that is so.

If the problem involves a statute, organize your answer by the statute's requirements and then the analytical classifications that courts have used to interpret the statute. For example, under Uniform Commercial Code § 2-302, a court may refuse to enforce an unconscionable contract. Courts usually analyze contracts attacked as unconscionable in terms of procedural and substantive unconscionability. Thus, you would organize your answer into each of these two categories. Then you would analyze the facts of the hypothetical according to the factors the courts have used to determine whether a contract is procedurally or substantively unconscionable.

Answering Specific Questions Specifically, and Providing Discussion

The traditional law school exam consists of a series of hypothetical questions. The professor will ask you to apply to those questions, in some fashion, the analytical framework you have learned in the course. Some of these questions will invite extended discussion, perhaps even upwards of an hour, while some questions may require much less time.

Besides in some way asking for discussion of a question of law, many exam problems will also pose a concrete legal issue, sometimes one that is procedurally focused. One example of such an issue would be, "Should the court grant the motion for a directed verdict"? At some point in your answer, and if possible at the beginning, *answer the specific question.*

Giving that answer, to be sure, is only one part of your task. Exam answers do not stop with a single word or phrase, unless they are multiple choice. In fact, most exam problems call for discussion. Therefore, you should engage in discussion. A stark question like whether a court should grant a particular motion usually implies, "Discuss," or "Analyze," or "Explain." Often the professor will use words like that. Yet, be sure to answer the bare question, too. One advantage of compelling yourself to do that is that it will force you into analysis of the problem, an analysis that should lead you into a discussion that exhibits your applied knowledge of the subject. Ultimately, for most professors, that analysis is more important than the answer yes or no.

Do Not Invent Facts

Most exam problems will include sufficient facts to stimulate discussion. The professor will have spent some time thinking about those facts, in order to test your ability to pull out relevant ideas from the course and apply them. Thus, a good general rule is, do not invent facts; use what is there. As an example, assume an exam problem that says that a man suffered great agony from a disease caused by a virus that escaped from a research facility, and clearly indicates that there was no negligence on the part of the owner of the facility. In analyzing this problem, you should concentrate on the question of whether there should be liability without fault in such a situation, and surely should not pause to discuss whether the owner of the facility was negligent. The exam tells you that there was no negligence, and therefore that is not an issue. The facts of the problem do directly present the issue of liability without fault, which is quite worthy of discussion. Moreover, although the virus caused great agony to the afflicted man, do not invent a family for him—a family not mentioned in the problem—and discuss whether they should be compensated for having to watch his pain. That would be inventing your own question, and your own issue, rather than those the professor presented.

There is at least one qualification to our warning against inventing facts. If the exam problem truly seems to lack an important fact, make an assumption and identify it as an assumption. This will show the professor that you are not trying to construct a better question than he or she did by making up facts, but also that, as a good lawyer should be able to do, you are able to state your premises.

Be Relevant

Be relevant. If there is a single piece of advice we would offer for writing exams—or for just about any lawyerly activity—that is it. This advice is easier preached than practiced. But it lies behind everything we have said to this point, and it applies as well to everything we say in the rest of the chapter. For common law claims, relevance means identifying and analyzing each element or factor of the claim. For statutory claims, relevance requires you to identify and analyze the particular statutory language at issue. In all cases, relevance requires that you identify the facts on which your analysis turns.

This advice merits a few examples.

1) The easiest case: Suppose your procedure exam includes a problem that ends with a specific question, "Rule on the motion for directed verdict and explain your ruling." Responding, you properly discuss the application of the law concerning directed verdicts to the hypothetical case in the exam. You set out the requirements for a directed verdict, and you analyze those requirements as they relate to the facts of the hypothetical, using analogies and distinctions from cases and examples you have studied. So far, so good. But then you decide you have not had enough to say. So you set out to write a comparison of motions for directed verdict with motions to dismiss, even though the problem has not indicated that there is any issue concerning the legal sufficiency of the complaint. That is not likely to win you any points. What you write about the motion to dismiss is irrelevant; it does not respond to the question. You would be better advised to check the question to assure yourself that you analyzed all facts and law necessary to rule on the motion for directed verdict. If you did, then you would be wise to spend on another part of the exam the precious minutes that you would otherwise waste on an irrelevant issue. A fundamental lesson, then, is to stick to the issue presented.

Look at the matter from the professor's point of view. She has given a problem that focuses on one issue and you have written an essay that includes another issue. If you were she, would you think the part of your answer concerning the other issue was relevant?

2) Suppose that in your contracts class, the professor presented four major ways for a person to impose liability on someone who has reneged on a promise or failed to live up to something analogous to a promise: a conventional offer-and-acceptance contract, promissory estoppel, moral obligation, and the theory of quasi-contract. Your contracts exam includes a problem that clearly, and only, presents the question of whether someone has accepted an offer. Because that

seems a little too simple, you mentally review all the theories of contract formation that you have studied. Although you decide that none of these really apply, you provide your instructor a learned little essay not only on offer and acceptance, but also on promissory estoppel, moral obligation and quasi-contract. At some point, your professor's eyes will glaze as she realizes that you are just listing things you have memorized and not applying them to the problem at hand.

Certainly, if the facts had raised any or all of the other three methods of recovery, discussion of those methods would be relevant. Indeed, if the facts gave you an opportunity to discuss all four of those methods, even if to explain why one or more don't apply, then you would discuss all four; that would be the difference between a good answer and a below average one. But when the facts do not fairly present an opportunity to discuss a particular rule or principle, you should not continue on in a way that does not address the problem at hand.

We would add that it is sometimes appropriate to make *assumptions* about facts that fairly could be inferred from a hypothetical even though they are not stated. A very simple example would be an exam problem in which A punches B. One clearly would want to analyze this as a problem in the law of battery, with the obvious conclusion that A had committed a battery. However, one might reasonably make the further assumption that A saw the punch coming, which would present the opportunity to discuss the tort of assault, which is an intentional act that places another in apprehension of an unprivileged contact. Most exam problems will not be as simple as that, and we cannot give you a pat formula to tell you when it is fair to make assumptions and when a particular professor will decide you have been appropriately creative in doing so. Still, most exam problems will provide you enough to analyze in a relevant manner that you should not waste time discussing issues that problems do not fairly present.

What we have been saying about relevance has strong practical application. Good lawyers can pick out the facts on which a question turns and apply what they know in ways that pertain to the question—that are relevant to the facts of that problem. We do not mean to suggest that there will not be times when there is a genuine issue as to relevance itself. Moreover, the presentation of an interesting angle on an issue that is really in an exam problem may earn you points, both for providing reasons to support your answers and for creativity. But we would not bank on credit for irrelevant discussions. Perhaps our principal single piece of negative advice about exam technique is that you should not throw the whole garbage can of your outline at every problem. Be selective about the law you apply and the facts that you analyze; that is the essence of relevance.

3) Some exam questions will require you to analyze statutory language, or language from documents such as contracts or wills, and to apply that language to the hypothetical facts of a problem. It is important that you first identify the particular language at issue from the statute or document. But, again, just identifying the issue is not enough. Next, explain how that language has been interpreted in the cases you have read for the course, including differing interpretations, and how each of those interpretations applies to the facts of the hypothetical. Then you should evaluate the interpretations.

For example, in an illustration at pages 67-68 that concerned a probate statute and a premarital contract and will, the issue was whether the testator had complied with the statutory language, "provision was made for the surviving spouse by settlement before or during marriage, or the survivor is provided for in the will." If the facts in that example were your exam question, you would identify the quoted language as the key to the issue, and discuss the cases you had read that interpreted the phrase "provision was made for the surviving spouse." Then you would analyze, in light of those cases, whether a premarital contract in which the parties agreed to give nothing to each other amounted to "provision" for the spouse.

Exam questions may involve more than one element or subsection of a statute or document, and may involve a combination of documents. Again, it is important to focus on the key language in each statute or document. For example, § 2-207(2) of the Uniform Commercial Code provides that new terms in an acceptance of a contract become part of that contract unless

(a) the offer expressly limits acceptance to the terms of the offer;

(b) they [the new terms] materially alter it; or

(c) notification of objection to them [by the offeror] has already been given or is given within a reasonable time after notice of them is received.

Now assume an exam question that takes place in a state that has adopted § 2-207(2). The question includes facts about a party's acceptance made on a form, and about the language of the offer and of the acceptance, in which the accepting party introduced new terms. The offer form does not include language that limits the offer to its terms. You would identify the issue as whether new language in the acceptance will become part of the contract. Your answer should then address each element of § 2-207(2), which is the rule in that state. You would observe quickly from the facts given that the offer was not expressly limited to its terms, so that the next issues are whether the new language in the acceptance materially altered the offer, and whether the offeror notified the accepting party of its objection in a reasonable time. Your answer would then discuss what you know about those two issues, applying the rules of subparts (b) and (c) of the statute to the facts given in the problem, and making analogies and distinctions from the case law you have read.

Some students think that they need only identify an issue—for example, in the UCC question we have just been discussing, that they need only say that if the new language materially alters the offer, the new terms are not part of the contract. To analyze an issue, however, you must go beyond identifying it. In the hypothetical, you should discuss whether the new terms do or do not materially alter the offer and *why*. In giving such a question on an exam, most professors will include facts that can be used to show why the new terms alter the offer, and also facts that can be used to show why the new terms do not alter the offer. Given such a question, you should weigh the competing sets of facts and arrive at the conclusion that seems most reasonable.

Get To the Point

Remember that time is precious when you are writing an exam, so you must get to the point. Ordinarily one should not begin answers to problems that focus on fact-based legal issues with graceful little essays about the background of the subject or about the great conflicting social interests it represents. That type of introduction may be appropriate if the question asks you only to discuss a particular policy or policies relevant to the course. But when answering a more traditional exam question, one should move directly into the *analysis* of the particular factual problem, although that analysis might well include relevant background about competing social interests.

An illustration of how you might achieve a blend between the facts of a problem and its social background, in one sentence, is this: "The argument against the defense of assumption of risk in workplace cases is that this defense was better suited to the days of its origin, when courts used it to protect infant industries." That way you have identified the issue—the applicability of the assumption of risk defense in cases involving worker injuries—but you also have set that issue in a framework of history and social policy. You have thus showed the professor your ability to engage in relevant analysis, rather than offering an exercise in casual essay writing.

Analyze and Establish Priorities

We now focus on analysis, which sometimes may seem an elusive idea, but is a technique you can learn for application to legal problems on exams. This Part will also reinforce advice we have previously given for application in other contexts, including legal writing generally. An initial point is that you should use your exam time according to the difficulty of a question or the number of particular issues in a question. If one part of a long and complicated question is that A punches B and B bleeds, state the battery issue crisply, resolve it by quickly explaining why A committed a battery, and move on without padding your answer on that simple point.

When you get to a more difficult issue, show that you understand its difficulty. Insofar as you have time, examine the hard issues from both sides, as a good judge would. Employ your tools of reason and persuasion to show why you think the court should resolve a close issue one way or the other. We present two examples of a fairly traditional approach that we think will prove useful in analyzing issues of some complexity; you probably will read or hear some different versions of this model.

Illustration: Street Harassment and Assault. Our first example is a case in which a construction worker, sitting on a wall at a building site during a coffee break, makes obscene propositions to a woman walking by, but does not get off the wall or make any kind of gesture. The woman sues the worker for assault, arguing on the basis of the evidence just summarized that she perceived a threat of unwanted physical contact. The defendant moves for a directed verdict after the presentation of this evidence.

A time-tested matrix for examination analysis includes these steps:

1) Identify the issue: Are obscene words that a listener perceives to threaten unwanted physical contact an assault if the words are not accompanied by acts or gestures? ·

2) State the "rule": The tort of assault requires three elements: (1) an act that (2) places the plaintiff in apprehension of (3) a harmful or offensive physical contact.

3) Apply the rule to the facts: Analyze each element. Although the plaintiff alleges that she apprehended a harmful or offensive contact, the defendant made no movement toward the plaintiff, indeed did not even gesture toward her. Because the defendant thus committed no act, the plaintiff's case at its strongest does not fulfill the first requirement of the definition of assault even if she could prove the second and third elements.

4) Draw a conclusion: The court should grant the defendant's motion for directed verdict, because under the law of assault, no reasonable person could find for the plaintiff.

This is a straight syllogistic way of proceeding. The major premise is the rule, the definition of assault. The minor premise stems from the facts, which crucially include the lack of an act. The conclusion is that there is no assault. Many people use an acronym known as IRAC (Issue, Rule, Analysis, Conclusion) to describe this method of organizing exam answers.

Beyond that stark conclusion, you might choose to elaborate a little about the rationales of the law, and the policy tensions in the case. Whether you do this, and how extensively you do it, will depend partly on how much time you have, and partly on your perception of the professor's hospitality to creative arguments. If the question is one for which the professor allots only a few minutes, keep your answer brief. If the examination allots more time, however, then the professor will expect you to analyze more deeply.

Although you have concluded that ultimately the plaintiff's case must fail, it would indicate your recognition of the difficulties the problem poses to observe that it is arguably unjust to allow vile words of this sort to go without a remedy. Having manifested that understanding, you might turn to a defense of the conclusion that the traditional definition of assault will bar the plaintiff's suit. Thus, you might point out that because of the First Amendment, the law is very cautious about attaching penalties to speech unaccompanied by acts. You also could argue that the requirement of an overt act makes the law administrable, since without that requirement, the judgment of whether there has been wrongful conduct might become too subjective. You might further declare that people in everyday life must develop tough hides, even about obscene comments, and conclude that the law cannot respond to every complaint arising from emotional reactions to the rough-and-tumble of ordinary existence. Finally, you might note that even though the law does not permit an assault action on these facts, some states conceivably might allow a suit for the tort of intentional infliction of emotional distress, which does not require that the defendant engage in an overt physical act.

By contrast, if there were time, you might consider the argument that in the circumstances of the hypothetical, the facts justify stretching the definition of assault to include words. After all, the movement of the lips and vocal cords required to make an obscene remark are literally an act. You might invoke a basic purpose for the tort of assault, which is to protect the interest in being free from apprehension of unwanted physical contacts. From that premise, you could argue that a woman in these circumstances could reasonably feel threatened and be apprehensive of an unwanted touching whether or not the defendant made an overt physical movement. Even if you took that position, however, you still might be inclined to conclude that the plaintiff must lose on assault, if for no other reason than maintaining that tort category as one that judges can administer with relative ease.

Our basic lesson is that for many issues, you will not want to stop with the syllogism. You will want to use analogies and policy arguments: to develop your analysis, to demonstrate that you understand the difficulty of a problem, and to show that you can weigh conflicting interests and arrive at a conclusion.

Illustration: Toxic Wastes and Liability Without Fault. A second illustration is a case that involves toxic wastes discharged by a large chemical company into ground water. The exam problem indicates that the defendant company used the best possible techniques for disposal of chemical wastes, and employed those techniques in a scrupulously careful manner. Despite the company's care, however, the chemicals leaked into the pond of a poor farmer who was farming on substandard acreage. As is the case with our virus hypothetical at page 175 above, a crucial question is whether the defendant should be liable without fault—without a showing that it was negligent. The strict liability tort that might apply to such a situation depends on the balancing of factors rather than being an "elements" cause of action like the tort of assault. Your answer might take the following form, identifying and analyzing those factors, which are listed on page 83.

> This problem involves an activity that presents a very high risk to a landowner when the defendant's activity is not clearly appropriate to the area. By hypothesis, the defendant's conduct is not negligent, because it observed the highest standard of care in the conduct of that activity. Another argument for the defendant is that to impose liability would violate the principle

that ordinarily a person should not have to compensate for harm caused without fault.

There are, however, countervailing principles of both ethics and economics that urge that those who create dangerous conditions that harm others should pay their own way. Requiring compensation from firms that discharge toxic chemicals would spread the costs of pollution—temporarily externalized on the farmer and those who consume his farm products—among those who benefit from the use of the chemicals.

Moreover, even if this argument did not entirely persuade the court, it is important that the farmer apparently has no practical means of defending his pond against the chemicals. The farmer's relatively defenseless position would support the imposition of liability on the chemical company even in the absence of fault. These considerations, together with what is arguably the inappropriateness of the defendant's activity, even in a rural community, lead me to conclude that strict liability should apply.

This example emphasizes policy arguments in addition to weaving in such factors as the high degree of risk, the plaintiff's vulnerability, and the inappropriateness of the activity in the environment; a more fleshed-out answer would draw on case law for the purposes of analogy or distinction. The example does provide an illustration of how you can train yourself to recognize difficult issues and then to discuss them in a way that indicates your recognition of the difficulties. Beyond that, please note that after "playing with" the problem, by contrasting both sides of the argument in relation to the facts, the writer of this answer came to a conclusion. That is a principal task of lawyers—attorneys have to argue for a concrete result; judges must decide a case.

Again, Be Concise

Concise writing is especially important when you write time-pressured examinations. As an example, let us say that you are dealing with the chemical wastes problem just discussed, but the question contains several other issues and you do not have time to write the three indented paragraphs above. A summary is all that is called for, or all you have time for. Here is a short paragraph that illustrates how you can compress ideas and save words and thus time.

> The defendant will argue that it should not be liable because it observed the highest standard of conduct, and that conducting such activities in the countryside rather than in urban areas provides a net benefit to society. However, the court should impose strict liability because of the unfairness of the pollution to the defenseless farmer and because requiring the company to compensate will appropriately spread the loss.

In this brief paragraph, we have provided: (1) An identification of the legal issue, plus (2) the policy argument for the defendant, in a way that shows respect for the argument, and (3) the policy argument for the plaintiff, leading right into (4) a conclusion. The use of "However" to begin the second sentence illustrates how you can use simple literary techniques—-here, a transitional word—that can help you pack a lot of meaning into a short paragraph.

Some Pitfalls to Avoid

Many teachers grade exams by assigning points to each issue in a question. The better you analyze an individual issue, the more points you get, up to a maximum number. This means that your exam-taking strategy should be to use your time in ways that will add points to your answer, including an effort to apportion your time efficiently among multiple issues, and surely to answer each question. Of course, the best way to maximize your score is by the quality of your answer, which is what much of this chapter has been about. However, you should also be aware of some ill-advised practices that take time and get you no points. For example:

- Don't repeat. Repetition will not add to your score. So, do not summarize your point in an introduction, then do a full analysis, and then repeat the introduction as a conclusion. You will be saying the same thing three times and getting points only once.
- Don't restate the facts. Of course, you should *use* the facts and analyze them. However, you need not begin your answer with a statement of facts as you would for a memorandum.
- Don't announce to the professor your situation concerning time. You need not explain at the end of your answer that your time is up or that the registrar is taking your paper. Your teacher will know that the end of your writing means that the time for the exam is over. Instead, use that extra sentence to write one last point analyzing the exam question.

Summing Up

For emphasis, we summarize a few things that impress professors when they grade examinations:

- Clear organization
- Identification of the issue
- Analyzing the issue, using the important facts
- Applying relevant legal rules to specific facts
- Applying broad policy ideas to concrete situations
- Identifying the arguments for and against a particular result and arguing persuasively to a conclusion
- Clear writing
- Concision

***

In conclusion, we first offer some advice about how to function after an exam, particularly if there are other exams to come. The gist of the lesson is, do not reflect on an exam after it is over. This may be an anti-intellectual suggestion, but for most students, it will be useful to preserve sanity.

If possible, avoid talking about the exam with other students. If you do, someone may ask about something you did not discuss—something like, "What did you do with the promissory estoppel issue in the case involving the uncle?" Reacting, horrified, "Oh my gosh, I never even saw a promissory estoppel issue," you will believe that your contracts grade is ruined. There are at least three reasons why you must not brood this way: 1) There may have been no promissory estoppel issue; your classmate may have been wrong; 2) If there was such an issue, the professor may not give it as much weight as your classmate thought it deserved; 3) One way or the other, you cannot do anything about it, and brooding about either uncertainty or perceived certainty of failure will make you unnecessarily miserable until the grades come out.

So move on. Go to a movie, or start studying for the next exam, if there is one. Get some sleep. This is almost compulsory advice if there is a next exam. Even if you have finished with a set of exams, we still suggest that you do not re-play the exam week in your mind. You cannot do anything about it. Enjoy whatever break time you have. If you have been lucky enough to get a summer job, concentrate on that.

Our final advice is to play your game as well as you can during the whole period of exams. By playing your game, we mean that you write up to the limits of your ability and knowledge, as well as the pressure of the moment allows. Consistency is the key. You will miss some issues and not discuss some others as fully as you would like. But even great basketball players miss free throws at crucial moments and even great golfers miss short putts late in the tournament. The key is consistency. Thus, shrug off what you perceive as mistakes and keep taking your free throws and hitting your putts. If you play your game, you will come out on your average, which is all any of us can ask.

15

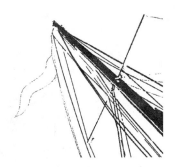

It's a Mind Game: Psychological Tips for the Study of Law

Law study puts mind, body, and emotions to the test.

This book principally aims to provide the most basic tool kit for the mind, but you should not neglect your physical and emotional well-being. The best one-word advice for dealing with the physical demands of law study is: exercise. How you specifically should act on this advice will depend in large part on your prior habits and life style. We do *not* suggest that if you have always been a couch potato, you should begin your first week of law school by running fast miles. We do think that even those whose main commitment to physical activity has been channel surfing will benefit from at least regular walking, built up by increments, as often as you have time to do it. If you are used to exercise, strenuous or otherwise, it is quite as important that you do not put away that part of your life, even if you do not continue to push yourself at your pre-law school level. The basic point is that you get some regular exercise, at what is a reasonable level for you, unless there is a medical reason not to do so. Your body and your mind will thank you for it.

There is a corollary concise suggestion: rest. Apart from defined exercise, get some rest and relaxation. Besides imposing a heavy workload, law school is stressful, and the combination of a lot of work and stress is fatiguing. This point requires emphasis for people whose prior lives have tended to ignore the need for relaxation as well as for sleep. No matter how important it may seem to do the extra half hour's work, consider listening to a favorite tape without a book in front of your nose, or observing the squirrels, or rapping, or even watching a lawyer show on television.

Building on our lengthy advice for the mind throughout the book, and our brief advice for the body just above, this chapter presents some ideas to help you overcome common psychological hurdles on the way to a law degree. We have culled these ideas from listening to students, and observing them, over a full generation of law study and teaching.

There Is Pressure in Law School

There is no denying that there is pressure in law school, particularly in the first year. If you have some significant experience in employment, you should be no stranger to some degree of pressure. Hard undergraduate work or demanding extracurricular activities may also have given you some toughening. However, even many people with work experience find that law school is especially taxing. Almost everything you encounter is new, much of it is confusing, and everything takes more time. Therefore, as a friend who is a clinical psychologist remarked, "You should feel that you have permission to feel overwhelmed."

There has been a lot of discussion over the years about whether law school needs to be as unpleasant as it is for many students. Derek Bok, a law professor who became dean of Harvard Law School and president of Harvard University, reflected on the question of whether the first year could be "done without the fear, without the doubts and the gnawing sense of inadequacy that often accompanies" that period of law study. He answered doubtfully, rationalizing that "one of the unpleasant but enduring truths in life is that most of our greatest personal advances, our most creative leaps, the times when we really move forward in our self-understanding and our self-awareness come from unhappy, stressful, and unpleasant experiences."[1]

---

[1] Derek Bok, Derek Bok IL, Harvard Law Bulletin, Fall 1995, 35 at 36.

Although we have mixed feelings ourselves about some of the harsher aspects of law school life, we think it appropriate to say that whatever your previous range of experiences, if you want to be a lawyer, you might as well get to used to pressure. A lawyer we know recently told us that when he interviews a student for a job, he is trying to project an image of her fifteen years ahead, to a time when she is a full-fledged lawyer. He pictures this person in the following situation: A client walks in, on the verge of tears, and tells the lawyer that the company he has built for twenty years is about to go down the drain because of its legal problems. He asks for her help, quickly. Now, that is pressure. When you find it useful to put the pressures of law school in perspective, you should consider that law school generally, and most professors, are less emotionally demanding than professional life.

A different perspective on the subject, emphasizing some aspects of law school about which you might ordinarily not think, appears in a letter from a lawyer to a university alumni magazine. This letter writer was responding to an article in which a law graduate complained bitterly about his law school experiences. In his response, the letter writer noted that he had come to law school immediately after finishing his service as a company commander in Vietnam. He declared that he was "profoundly grateful during every single day of my three years at [Harvard Law School] that (a) it was conducted indoors; (b) I had the luxury of devoting my time wholly to reading, writing, discussion and other purely intellectual activities; and (c) no one was trying to kill me."[2]

If you have led a relatively sheltered life, the pressures of law school may be more daunting than they were to this Vietnam veteran. However, there are ways to cope with those pressures. We have already suggested the two simplest and most practical, to get rest and exercise. Another coping strategy is this: keep up your relationships with family and friends. In fact, make new friends, just as you have all your life. Some of the friends you make in law school may even turn out to be professional assets, but make friends for whatever reasons you have always made them.

Keep in mind, finally, that it is not a mark of weakness to seek

---

[2] David C. Carrad, Letter, in Harvard Magazine, May-June 1995, at 7.

help when you need help. All law schools have personnel designated to help you over personal and family crises and to guide you to counselors or therapists if you begin to feel overwhelmed. Professors, even if they are not therapeutically trained, can usually offer some help and can at least put you on the track to the right people. If you think that your feelings of inadequacy or anxiety are really beyond normal limits, do not hold back. Let someone know about your problems.

Preserving Your Humanity

Despite the ferocious image of law school conveyed by the media, fiction, and general rumor around campus, we think that law students tend to be decent folks. Moreover, even if there are a few piranhas, you can exert a lot of influence on who you choose to deal with—as friends, acquaintances, or study group members. However, you do want to stay alert to the challenge that the competitive aspect of law school poses to one's humanity.

Since law students learn early that hours and even quarter hours are precious, part of the challenge to your good instincts has to do with how you spend your time. A heartening example is one talented student in both of our first-year classes who put in a considerable amount of time helping another student, whose first language was not English, practice for an oral argument. The same student also spent a significant amount of time psychologically buoying up another classmate who had been diagnosed with a serious disease. P.S. The altruistic student did pretty well his first year and went on to become editor-in-chief of the Law Review.

It is true that difficult problems of choice will arise, presenting local versions of age-old moral conflicts. Here is a hypothetical drawn from more than one real-life situation. Sam is a third-year student who is a member of the Law Review. As a help to its members, many of whom skip a lot of classes to do their work for the publication, the Review maintains a bank of outlines for upper-year courses. This batch of outlines has been developed over the years, and has no identifiable authors. These outlines are thus not like study group outlines, primarily written by one person or by a very small group for the group. Still, it is the custom of the Review that the outlines are meant only for Review members.

Martha, Sam's wife, is a second-year student who is taking a course covered by one of the outlines. Should Sam share a Law Review outline with Martha, who is not a Review member? Do you find it amazing that this issue even poses a problem? We can only put the question. When law school challenges one morality with another, you will have to make choices about your personal priorities.

Having left that question to you, we will underline some previous advice. On some days of law school, even in some weeks, the pressure of work will pretty much cause you to lose touch with your family and your friends. Try not to let that become a habit. The reason is not only that it is "doing the right thing" to make time for those to whom you are closest. It is that they want to help you, and can do so only if they understand the process you are living through. A disposition to talk about that process will benefit both you and them. They will feel more a part of your life, and you will be able to unburden yourself more easily.

Echos of the Paper Chase: The "Socratic Method" And Feeling Put Down by the Professor

There aren't many professors left, if there ever were very many, like Professor Kingsfield, the tyrannical Contracts teacher of the movie and TV show *The Paper Chase*. But that does not change the fact that the atmosphere of some law classrooms is intimidating to many students, and may manifest itself in student psychology in the feeling that the professor has delivered a put down.

To deal with this kind of reaction, you have to understand that a lot of law is about argument. That is evident when you think about the litigation side of the law. Even in nonlitigation branches of the profession, however, you sometimes will have to do some argu-ing—if only with yourself—in order to serve your client. For example, if you are preparing the legal end of a business deal, you must keep posing "What if" questions to yourself in order to consider the implications of a proposed course of action and to protect your client. People who engage in legal planning often benefit by challenging their own initial analyses. In that sense, testing out your ideas against yourself—or having a partner argue with you to make sure that you have considered all the angles—is part of being a lawyer.

We hope that your professors will employ this technique in *true* socratic style, putting questions that inspire you to think through the implications of your position. Thus, when the professor asks what may seem to you a put down question, you should think of the question as a way to make you think. That is really all most professors are trying to do when they use a questioning style of instruction—make you think. We understand that sometimes the method comes across as a professor's self-satisfied triumph. However, if you learn what the teacher wants you to learn, the triumph will be yours.

Most importantly, you should understand that this form of argument is not personal. In the socratic classroom situation, the student who must personally respond to the instructor's questions is just a representative of his or her colleagues, one through whom the professor develops ideas that are important to the class.

Of course, in a class of one hundred and twenty, or even twenty, it will seem embarrassing if you give the "wrong" answer. But remember that the professor is concentrating on developing the lesson, and, a day later, probably will not even recall what you said. Even if she does, she may think your "wrong" response was more acute than you gave it credit for. In general, the only answers professors tend to associate with particular students are the brilliant ones. Remember also that if you are confused about a class, or want to test out your understanding of a subject, or just want to get a better sense of your professor, you can always go to his or her office and talk about the material.

If you are concerned about what other students may have thought of an alleged little "mistake," consider that your remarks in class are subject to a lot of competition in their own minds. They may be struggling with the material so hard they barely hear you. They may be concocting fabulous answers of their own. They may be thinking about their sick spouse or child. So please understand, for your own mental health, that your "wrong" answer was not as much the center of the universe as you thought.

The Awesome Other Student

There is an analogous point about the responses that other students give in class. Sometimes other students will sound like Holmes, Brandeis, and Cardozo all rolled into one. We will offer some explanations for the psychology of this phenomenon.

Often students who speak in class—at least volunteers—are speaking because they have thought about a problem, or perhaps have done a little extra reading on it, and because they think they have something special to contribute. Thus, students who speak up are self-selected; they are giving out what they at least consider the cream of their thought on a subject.

The responses of several of these students may tend to blend in your mind into one Awesome Other Student. We speculate that you may put together in your own mind the best responses that six or eight students can give, and associate all those answers with the hypothetical person of one enormously talented individual. If your anxiety level rises, you may get to thinking that every other student in the class is the Awesome Other Student—everyone but you is capable of distilling in his or her mind the greatest wisdom possessed by the best prepared and most aggressive group of students in the class on any one occasion.

This perception is false. Even if it were true, there would be nothing you could do about it. But it is not true. You should not make yourself feel inferior to the Awesome Other Student, because that student does not exist. Just play your game and think through things as well as *you* can; that is all you can ask of yourself in any event.

Yet, we should add that playing the game does include listening to what other students have to say. Sometimes their remarks will be sensible and even penetrating; often they will at least make you think. Moreover, now and then, there will be a genuinely talented person in the class whose answers make sense, time after time. Do not be envious, and do not be daunted. Learn from that person. Even if this genius happens to be arrogant about his or her talent, recognize it for what it is: a gift. One of the authors was in several classes with a very bright and verbal student, and took notes on everything he said. We would add that you should not judge talent prematurely. What may seem an incomparably fine mind in September may appear less scintillating by April—and the other way around.

Resentment and Alienation

Sometimes law school breeds resentments and alienation. There is, in fact, a scholarly literature that has developed about these phenomena. But in part, they are an outgrowth of some very positive developments. For example, a generation ago, there was no concern that women and minorities felt alienated from a law school culture that was overwhelmingly white and male. The reason there was no concern was that there were few women or minorities in law schools. One of us cannot recall a single African-American, and can remember only a few Latinos, in a large law school when he began teaching in 1965. When the other was a member of a law review in 1975, every one of the dozen top editors was male and she was one of only eight women out of a total of 76 members of the Review.

It is not surprising that as groups previously excluded from the process of legal education have moved into law school, new tensions have arisen. Many women complain about what they regard as male domination of both the content of legal rules and the perspective of the classroom. Minorities view themselves as marginalized by a lack of attention to the experiences that have shaped their lives. White males themselves resent what they perceive as employment preferences given to females and minorities.

The strife extends even to pronouns, as uses of "he" and "she" become occasions for criticism. Male students may get tired of professors, both women and men, who seem to hypothesize only female judges, just as female students have thought that too many of their professors talk only about males. Backlashes and overreactions abound.

These diverging views in law schools are certainly not unique, and they reflect changes in society as a whole. We could say that everyone should "celebrate diversity" and leave it at that. Instead, we will indicate that one of the best things law school can do for you is to teach you to judge people, as well as ideas, on their merits, and to see that their merits may be diverse ones.

What Does the Professor Want?

We refocus on the professor. When you are not thinking that he is putting you down, you may be saying to yourself, "What does he want?" Sometimes a student will say that right out in class: "I don't know if this is what you're after." Well, sometimes the professor is not entirely clear himself. He probably does have a goal in mind—an idea that he wants to work around to. But, particularly if he is learning the subject himself—or rethinking it—he may not have a firm idea of "the answer."

Whatever is in the professor's mind, our advice is to relax a little. If you are the subject of the teacher's questioning, bend with the questions. Let the discussion sift itself out. At any point in the dialogue, all you can do is try to answer the one question on the floor. If you are not clear, ordinarily the professor will rephrase. Eventually, there probably will be progress. At worst, most class hours are only 50 minutes long. If you are not the subject of the professor's questions, take notes on them. Some of your most valuable notes may be those questions, rather than answers.

As you try to understand the questioning method used in many law school classrooms, or at least to cope with it, you may find it useful to consider the way that you learn things generally. Most of the important things you learn in life do not come by rote memory. Often you learn them by problems being posed to you, forcing you to think, and by repetition of analogous and progressively more difficult problems. These lessons frequently emerge from various forms of dialogue, which eventuate in you saying, perhaps to yourself, "*Now* I see." That is the law school classroom, at least in the socratic form, at its best. If a particular class in which you find yourself does not measure up to that ideal, grin and bear it. But stay with the questioning. You might learn something.

It's the Question

What we have just said leads us to reemphasize a truth that is often difficult for students to accept: the questions are frequently more important than the answers.

One thing that you may grumble off and on—along with "She put me down" and "What is she looking for?"—is, "Why doesn't she give us the rule? She knows the rule. Let her give it to us."

When you indulge that complaint, you are missing the point. Especially in the first year of law school, the rules are not Einsteinian physics. We do not say they are easy, but it is the process of formulating questions that poses the greatest challenge. Thus, law school tends to concentrate on imparting a method for putting the questions—stating the issue, as it is called.

It is true that you cannot see an issue unless you have learned enough about the rules to understand that an issue exists. For example, if you do not know the elements of the tort of assault, it will be difficult for you to pose the precise question of whether vile words unaccompanied by an act can be an assault. However, you will not be able to function as a law student, let alone as a lawyer, unless you are able to identify an issue. Without the issue you have no need for a rule, and without the rule, you have no occasion for discussion. That is why the questions truly are often more important than the answers.

The Professor Can Be Wrong

Now we offer some balm for the bruises you may think you sustained when a professor "put you down": The Professor Can be Wrong. Different professors will react in different ways, mostly according to their personalities, to the question of how subversive this statement is.

However subversive, it is true. Naturally, though, you will have to gauge your professor in deciding how much you want to argue about ideas he has expounded that seem clearly mistaken. People call that prudence.

To place the matter at a particularly crucial juncture, when you are writing exams, you will have to make judgments about how hospitable individual professors are likely to be to arguments that do not agree with their basic premises. That is *certainly* prudence. Frankly, there are a few professors who have a view of their subject that is so set in concrete that they honestly cannot see a fair argument on the other side, or even another way to define the problem. Humor them. Or at least, humor them on the exam, enough to view the problem as they would view it. Understand, however, that you do not have to give up your private assessment of a legal problem, which may include a judgment that the professor is wrong.

Remember that a successful legal education should prepare you to assess ideas on their merits. As a lawyer, you will have to do that all the time, and sometimes entirely on your own. Thus, do not view the professor with a different viewpoint as a capricious roadblock to understanding. View him as a way to challenge your own ideas, to discard those that are not as good as his, and at least privately to validate those ideas of yours that you believe—after reflection—are better ones. More generally, view him as a vehicle for helping you to enhance your own intellectual independence.

A Conclusion

We conclude with a few remarks about what law school should do, what it does do, and how generally to cope with the process of legal education. Law school should make you better—intellectually richer, mentally sharper, psychologically more sensitive to a variety of viewpoints, more practiced and more secure in dealing with situations involving conflict.

It actually will do all of these things. However, there are likely to be times when the process will get you down. Sometimes a particular trigger will be your belief that you gave a foolish answer in class. Or it may be the heavily edited paper that comes back to you on your first legal writing assignment—especially a shock because your prior teachers assured you all through high school and college that you write like a dream. Or it may be a disappointing set of examination grades. To Derek Bok, the Harvard Law School student who became dean of that school and then president of the university, it was his grades on midyear practice exams: "I was sure I would flunk out."

You will have to work your way through episodes like these as best as your psychological resources permit. You can be assured that at some time or another, a majority of your classmates will share these feelings of inadequacy or vexation. Surely, you should not forget how your own resilience has carried you through past difficulties.

Having presented several practical therapeutic suggestions in this chapter, often simply by way of explaining the goals of the process, we offer a few parting comments and exhortations.

- Life tends to reward effort.
- In any event, effort produces its own intrinsic reward.
- Grades are not your measure as a human being.
- Humor provides both perspective and relief.
- You can do only your best, and only you can decide what your best is.
- Life is a marathon, and early leaders are not always winners.
- Only you can decide what "winning" is—that is, only you can determine the measure of success.

We hope you have a rewarding, and even enjoyable, three years.